SOAP RECIPES

**Seventy tried-and-true ways
to make modern soap
with herbs, beeswax and
vegetable oils**

ELAINE C. WHITE
Illustrated by James Tollett

Valley Hills Press
1864 Ridgeland Road
Starkville, MS 39759 USA
(601) 323-7100

W9-CFJ-695

Illustrations by James Tollett
Graphic design by William Pitts
Photographs by Jimmy Cole
          and Elaine C. White

If you have any questions or comments concerning this book, please write or call the publisher:
Valley Hills Press
1864 Ridgeland Drive
Starkville, MS 39759 USA
Telephone/Fax. (601) 323-7100

White, Elaine C.
    Soap recipes : seventy tried-and-true ways to make modern soap with herbs, beeswax & vegetable oils / Elaine C. White.
    p. cm.
    Includes bibliographical references and index.
    Preassigned LCCN: 94-90605
    ISBN 0-9637539-5-9

    1. Soap   I. Title.

TT991.W47 1995   668'.124
                                  QBI94-2373

This book is dedicated to those
who experienced misfortune
because they followed
a bad soap recipe.

Acknowledgments

The author expresses her gratitude to the following people who helped with the research and publication of **Soap Recipes**:

Mabel Barker of Barker Enterprises™ provided professional advice about waxes and donated waxes for research.

Thanks to Jd Belanger, Editor of *Countryside & Small Stock Journal* (who "passed the word"), Paulette Wohnoutka of Humansville, Missouri provided goat fat and Martha Philipps of Bloomfield, Indiana provided sheep fat for the development of soap recipes.

Pourette Manufacturing® provided the artwork on page 25 and technical information about aniline dye.

The Rosemary House provided friendly service and donated henna for the development of castile shampoo.

Sunfeather Herbal Soap Company™ provided the artwork on page 66.

Wil White and John Langberg shared their expertise.

About the author

Elaine C. White is an award-winning cook, winemaker and beekeeper. She is the author of numerous magazine articles about crafting with honey and beeswax and known to many as a "honey and beeswax craft specialist."

Soap Recipes is Elaine's second book. Her first book, also published by Valley Hills Press, is entitled ***Super Formulas, Arts and Crafts:*** *How to make more than 360 useful products that contain honey and beeswax.*

Joyce Elaine Carpenter-White was born January 29, 1952 in Starkville, Mississippi, where she currently lives with two computer enthusiasts: her husband, Wil, and son, John.

Preface

During the summer of 1993, I discovered a computer bulletin board service dedicated to chemistry. On the board, I asked questions and tried to learn the secrets of successful soapmaking. Luckily, many chemists took time to translate "soap alchemy" into terms I could understand. What they didn't know, they researched, translated into nonprofessional terms and passed along to me. Those chemists deserve a lot of credit for the development of this book. They provided the answers I needed to develop and test the soap recipes.

Based on test results, I selected only the best recipes and present them in this book.
I explain soapmaking in the simplest terms I know. I hope *Soap Recipes* is the missing link between modern chemistry and the amateur soapmaker at home.

May all your soap "bee" perfect,

Elaine C. White

Contents

Illustrations by James Tollett
Graphic design by William Pitts
Photographs by:
    Jimmy Cole pages 33, 34, 37, and 168
    Elaine C. White all other photographs

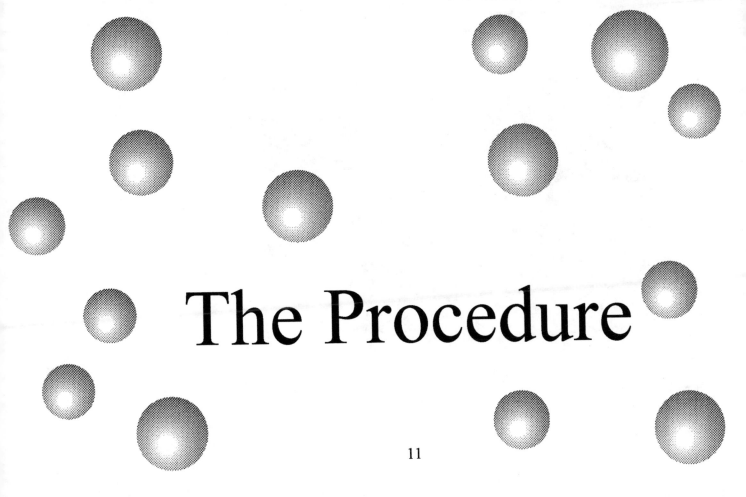

The Procedure

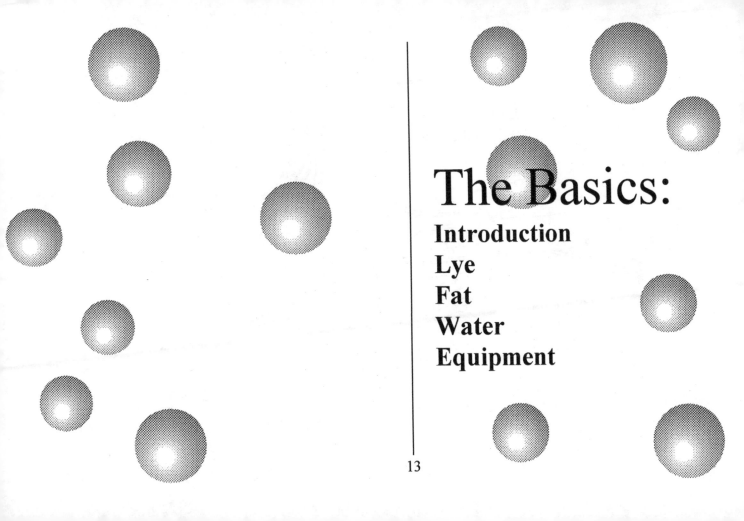

The Basics:

Introduction
Lye
Fat
Water
Equipment

Introduction

Let's make soap! There are many reasons to make your own soap. The first reason that comes to mind is economy. Certainly, it can be less expensive to make your own and that's why many begin. If you embark on the road to soapmaking because you like good soap, you'll soon discover that quality, variety and independence are the reasons you continue to make soap. In essence, you've given yourself the opportunity to make the kind of soap that you like.

Reading this book and learning the fundamentals will give you a foundation to express yourself unendingly in what you make. The best soap in the world is the one you made. The knowledge to make soap awards you with a glowing sense of accomplishment.

Making quality soap is easy! Don't let anyone tell you otherwise. At the same time, making bad soap is easy, too. Our great-grandparents made soap with lye from wood ashes. The lye strength was hard to judge and the resulting soap was very unpredictable.

The development of commercial lye led to a safer, more accurate way of making soap at home. Today, there are many bad soap recipes in print. Bad recipes account for most soapmaking failures. Failures make people think that soapmaking is difficult or that home made soap is inferior to commercially made soap—which isn't true!

Maybe you're a bit anxious and wonder whether it is possible to make good soap. Anyone can make good soap as long as they have a good recipe and know the little things that make a big difference in soap. I'll give you good recipes and I'll tell you "the little things." You'll be proud of the soap that you make from the recipes in this book.

Here's an outline of the soapmaking procedure. You need three ingredients to make soap: lye, fat and water. Dissolve the lye in water and add the lye-water to the fats. A chemical reaction, called saponification, turns fat and lye into soap and glycerin. The reaction begins when you first combine the lye and fat. With time, the mixture turns opaque and thickens.

While the soap is still thin enough, pour it into molds, where the thickening process continues. After a day or two in the molds, remove the soap and place it where air can circulate about it for three or four weeks. During this time the chemical reaction continues; the soap becomes harder, milder and ready for use. Sound simple?—It is! Ready to try?—Okay!

Lye

The most important and misunderstood soap ingredient

Soap is made from lye, fat and water. You're probably familiar with fat and water, but not so familiar with lye. It can be nasty when handled improperly. If you can get past the following warnings about lye, you are destined to make soap.

Where to find lye

Look where drain cleaners are sold and buy 100% lye. Don't bother looking at liquid drain cleaners. You want 100% lye in granular form. Red Devil™ is one brand. Do not try Drain-O® because it contains particles of metal! If you can't be sure the drain cleaner is 100% lye, then order lye from a soap-making company or a laboratory supplier. Laboratory suppliers list lye flakes as "sodium hydroxide (tech)" and as "NaOH (caustic soda)."

Lye can react with metal.

Lye reacts with some metals. It should never contact zinc, iron, aluminum or tin. Safe containers include heat-proof stoneware, glass, enamel, stainless steel and heat-resistant plastic.

Lye plus water equals heat.

Mix lye with cold water and the mixture generates heat. It is important to use cold water and a container that can withstand temperatures up to 200 degrees F.

Lye is caustic!

Lye can be fatal if swallowed. Keep it out of the hands of children.

Paint remover?

Lye can remove paint. If lye, lye-water or freshly made soap splatters onto a painted surface, wipe it off immediately. Wash the area with water and detergent; wash it with clear water; then, wipe it dry.

Relax!

As I said before, if you can get past the warnings about lye, you are destined to make soap. I'll admit that the warnings sound frightening. Just remember that the only way lye can harm you is by contact. Burns from lye, lye-water and freshly made soap are not instantaneous. It takes awhile for lye to irritate skin. Chances are you will notice if lye splashes on you. You'll notice itching before burning. Lye-water on skin is first noticed by a slippery feeling. Rinse you hands with vinegar and immediately rinse them with running water. You should have no problems making soap.

Why would anyone want to use soap that contains something harsh as lye?

Well, the good news is that handmade soap *is made with lye*, but it doesn't actually *contain lye*—there's a difference. Lye reacts with fats to create approximately three molecules soap and one molecule glycerin. The lye is no longer in its nasty form, but converted to something wonderful. Handmade soap is approximately one-fourth glycerin. Glycerin is soothing to skin.

Fat
The fat guys

You can make soap from almost any fat.

The type of fat used to make soap provides versatility in soapmaking. Liquid vegetable oils are 100% fat. I refer to oils and fats (liquid and solid) as "fat."

White coconut oil is the fat used most often in these recipes. It contributes good lathering properties. Companies sell yellow coconut oil that contains butter flavor and color. If white coconut oil isn't available, you may substitute the yellow oil.

Fats were tested and not used in the recipes because of the objectionable odors they contribute to soap: clarified butter fat, cottonseed oil and raw linseed oil.

Substituting fats

Many people believe they can substitute any fat for the specific fat listed in soap recipes. This is wrong! Please don't substitute in these recipes. Here's an example of fat substitution that shows why it is *not* a good idea.

If you substitute olive oil for coconut oil:
1 pound coconut oil needs 2.9 ounces lye
  1 pound olive oil needs 2.2 ounces lye
Excess lye .7 ounces

This means the soap has .7 ounces excess lye which makes it unnecessarily harsh to skin. I repeat, please don't substitute fats in these recipes. Okay, now that you know the rule, here is the exception. The following oils require the same amount of lye; they may be combined and used interchangeably in the recipes. Just remember, if you substitute oils, you no longer have a tested recipe. The soap could take longer to thicken and turn out quite different.

Oils that can be used interchangeably	
avocado oil	safflower oil
canola oil	soybean oil
corn oil	sunflower oil
light sesame oil	sweet almond oil
olive oil	walnut oil
peanut oil	wheat germ oil

Water
A hard case of soap scum, bathtub ring and rigid laundry

High soil concentrations of limestone and gypsum cause hard water. Rainwater dissolves small amounts of minerals as it percolates through the soil. Ground-water in areas rich in minerals tends to be high in calcium carbonate, which makes water "harder" to use. In hard water, soap products form insoluble greases, called "soap film" or "soap scum."

What to do

If you live in an area with hard water, you probably know it because you've heard friends and neighbors talk about it. If you would like to test your water, kits are available from Chem Lab Supplies and Earth Guild (see Appendix K, page 196).

Lye reacts with minerals in hard water, lessening its strength for the soapmaking process. If your water supply is hard, use soft water such as rain water or distilled water to make soap. You'll also have to use soft water anytime you use soap.

When hard water problems are limited to stiff laundry or minor kettle scaling, one-third cup vinegar to each gallon of water can reduce hardness. Serious hard water problems require brine-regenerated ion-exchange water softeners.

If your water supply is hard, use rain water or distilled water to make and use soap.

Quick list of equipment

Here's a list of equipment necessary to make soap. You may already have everything! First, a quick list and then, the same list in more detail.

- one 4-to-6-cup stainless steel mixing bowl or pan
- one heat-proof container that holds at least 2 cups (Pyrex® is good)
- a rubber spatula
- two thermometers
- eye protection
- rubber gloves
- scales to weight the fats and lye
- soap molds
- a clock with a second hand or other type timer
- wire whisk (for some recipes)
- pot holders or oven mitts
- stainless steel measuring spoons

Equipment list in detail

- **One 4-to-6-cup stainless steel mixing bowl or pan**

Lye reacts with some metals. It should never contact zinc, iron, aluminum or tin. Safe containers include heat-proof stoneware, glass, enamel, stainless steel and heat-resistant plastic.

I used a stainless steel mixing bowl for the recipe tests. If you choose another type container, it could affect the time soap takes to thicken. For instance, heat-proof stoneware is very thick and heavy. It retains heat that can extend the time soap takes to thicken.

- **One heat-proof container that holds at least 2 cups**

When lye mixes with cold water, it generates heat. It is important to use cold water and a container that can withstand temperatures up to 200 degrees F.

- **A rubber spatula**

It takes a lot of stirring to make soap. I like to use a rubber spatula because it's easy to scrape the sides of the mixing bowl. Lye doesn't affect rubber, but the rubber tends to absorb the fragrance of essential oils. Once you use a rubber spatula to stir soap, don't use it again to stir food.

You can stir soap with a wooden spoon. Wood also absorbs fragrances and should not be used to stir food. Lye weakens wood fiber. After making many batches of soap, the spoon will gradually wear away. (The small slivers of wood fiber goes into the soap!) When the wood weakens enough, the spoon will break.

- **Two thermometers**

You need two thermometers: one for the lye-water and one for the fats. Each thermometer should measure as low as 90 degrees F and as high as 250 degrees F. It should be made of glass or stainless steel to withstand lye. Most candy and meat thermometers are glass or stainless steel.

When you heat fat, never rest the thermometer on the bottom of the container. Direct contact with heat makes the thermometer register a much higher temperature than the actual temperature of the fat.

Read the instructions that come with the thermometer. Many thermometers need three to five minutes to register the correct temperature. Instant-read thermometers are available and I highly recommend them.

- **Eye protection and rubber gloves**

It's easy to splatter soap while mixing it. Eye protection is vital! Wear sunglasses if you have to!

Rubber gloves are optional. I suggest you wear them to make the first few batches of soap—at least until you're comfortable with the process and confident in handling lye and freshly made soap. I no longer wear gloves to make soap. I *always* wear eye protection.

- **Scales to weigh the fat and lye**

Scales are a necessary part of successful soapmaking. Recipes by fluid measure (cups, heaping tablespoons, etc.) are not as accurate as recipes by weight. Fluid measure can become complicated. (I don't think you would appreciate it if recipes called for 1 cup, plus 1 tablespoon, plus 1 1/2 teaspoons fat!) There's another problem with

measures. One tablespoon lye in granular form contains more lye than one tablespoon of lye in flake form.

Since it takes a very small amount of lye to make soap, accurate scales are important. Electronic scales with a digital display and accuracy ±.1 ounce are perfect. When you shop for scales, try to find one that weighs increments as small as one-tenth of an ounce and as much as four pounds. Two companies that sell electronic scales with digital read-outs are Quill Corporation and Chem Lab Supplies (addresses at Appendix K, page 195).

• Soap molds

Properly made soap releases easily from any flexible mold that is clean (dry and oil-free). We are lucky to have plastic soap molds on the market and I believe in using them. I highly recommend the molds manufactured by Pourette.® Currently, there are no soap molds on the market that are as heat-resistant and durable.

Many molds contain six compartments. Use scissors to cut the molds in half. This results in two molds with three compartments each. Handling the mold is much easier. You don't have to buy molds. Plastic tubs, such as those that contain soft margarine spread, make good soap molds. Any flexible plastic container works well.

Guess what's new and fun to do? Pourette soap molds just for you!

Wendy Wick is a registered trademark of Pourette Manufacturing Company

25

- **A clock with a second hand**

The recipes list specific times to stir soap. A timer or a clock with a second hand should be within your view.

- **Wire whisk**

Stir the soap with a rubber spatula unless the recipe specifies that you should use a whisk. Most kitchen whisks are stainless steel and not affected by lye. Whisks are sometimes necessary to break up clumps or to get a smooth mixture. Splatters are more likely when you stir soap with a whisk. Keep a wet cloth nearby to clean up splatters and always wear eye protection.

- **Pot holders or oven mitts**

Pot holders or oven mitts are sometimes necessary to protect your hands from the heat of the lye-water and the soap.

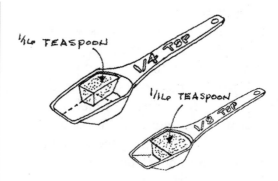

- **Stainless steel measuring spoons**

Fragrant oils can melt some types of plastic. Stainless steel measuring spoons are long-lasting and not affected by coloring powder or fragrant oil. Try to find a set that includes a 1/8-teaspoon measure. Some recipes require 1/16-teaspoon of an ingredient. To measure 1/16 teaspoon, estimate one half of a 1/8-teaspoon measure or estimate one fourth of a 1/4-teaspoon measure.

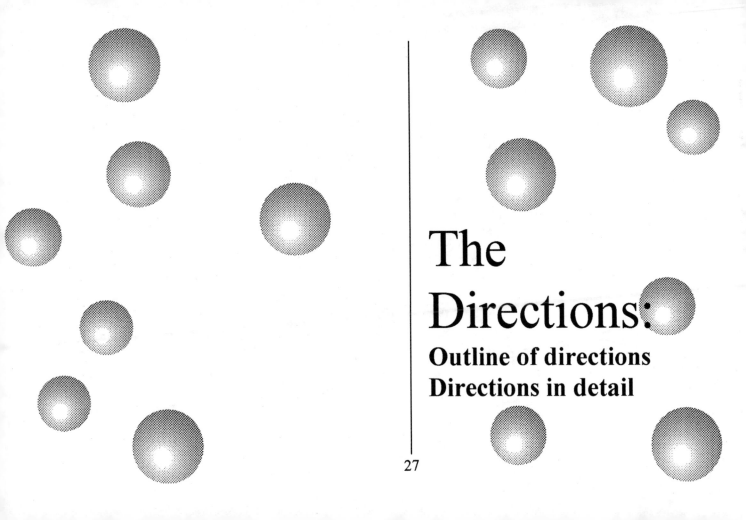

The Directions:

Outline of directions
Directions in detail

Outline of directions

There is one basic procedure to make any kind of soap. Let's go through the directions briefly. Don't worry about any terms you don't understand. I'll explain the steps (and the terms) later.

Step 1: Put the fats and optional ingredients in a stainless steel mixing bowl or pan. Heat them to the temperature specified as "fat temperature" in the recipe.

Step 2: Put on eye protection and rubber gloves.

Step 3: Dissolve the lye in cold water and wait for it to reach the temperature specified as "lye-water" in the recipe.

Step 4: When both the fat and lye-water reach the temperatures specified in the recipe, add the lye-water to the fat.

Step 5: Stir for the time specified as "tracing time" in the recipe.

Step 6: Add the fragrant oil and stir.

Step 7: Pour the soap into molds and wait the time specified as "time in molds" in the recipe.

Step 8: Unmold the soap.

Step 9: Wait the time specified in the recipe for soap to "age."

Step 10. Enjoy your soap!

**Sound simple?—It is!
Let's go over the steps in more detail and define those unfamiliar terms.**

29

Directions in detail

Step 1: Put the fats in a stainless steel mixing bowl or pan and heat them to the temperature specified as "fat temperature" in the recipe.

Put the fats in a stainless steel bowl or pan. Place a glass or stainless steel thermometer in the fats. (Be sure it doesn't touch the bottom of the container and give a false reading.) Unless the recipe specifies otherwise, add optional ingredients (such as herbs and cereals) to the fats. Heat the fats and optional ingredients to the temperature specified in the recipe.

Step 2: Put on eye protection and rubber gloves.

If lye, lye-water or freshly made soap splatters on your skin, there is plenty of time to rinse it off before it begins to burn. Wear gloves or not; it's your decision. Eye protection is a different matter entirely. Since lye burns skin, you can imagine what it does to eyes. It's difficult to rinse your eyes while they're burning and you can't see. This painful and dangerous situation is entirely avoidable. *Always wear eye protection!*

Step 3. Dissolve the lye in cold water and wait for it to reach the temperature specified as "lye-water temperature" in the recipe.

Use a heat-proof container (like a Pyrex® measuring cup) to measure the amount of cold water (70 to 75 degrees F) specified in the recipe. Cold water is important. If you add lye to hot or boiling water, the water could "boil-up" out of the container; if you add lye to *really* cold water (below 60 degrees F) the lye-water might not reach the high temperatures required to make some of the recipes.

Stir the water with a rubber spatula and slowly add the lye. The water will get hot and turn cloudy. Continue to stir until the lye dissolves. Don't breathe or intentionally smell the fumes coming from the cup, because they are quite "chokey." (Take my word for it.)

If you wait too long to stir the water, the lye could harden in the bottom of the container. This is not a problem. You can still stir it, but it will be more difficult.

Add a glass or stainless steel thermometer to the lye-water and wait until it reaches the temperature specified in the recipe for "lye-water temperature."

Step 4. When both the fat and the lye-water reach the temperatures specified in the recipe, add the lye-water to the fat.

It's sometimes a balancing act to get the fat mixture and the lye-water to specific temperatures at the same time. Never place lye-water in a microwave! I broke two measuring cups that way before I realized what was happening.

It takes lye-water longer to cool than it takes fat to heat. I usually wait for the lye-water to cool to about five degrees F above the desired temperature, then heat the fat on a stove.

When both the fat and the lye-water reach the temperatures specified in the recipe, use a pot holder and move the bowl to a sink (to contain splatters). Pour the lye-water into the fat. It doesn't matter if you pour it in slowly or quickly. Just relax and pour it any way you like.

Step 5. Stir for the time specified as "tracing time" in the recipe.

When lye, water and fat first combine, the mixture is thin and watery. Gradually, as the lye and fat react chemically to form soap, the mixture thickens and turns opaque. "Tracing" is a term to describe the consistency (thickness) of soap when it's ready to pour into molds.

Tracing is absolutely necessary if you plan to add herbs or other powdered additives to soap. If you pour a thin soap mixture that contains additives into molds, the additives may sink or float. When you re-move the soap from the mold, you'll find that most of the additives are on the top, bottom, or edges of the bar. Soap should trace before you pour it into molds so those wonderful additives stay evenly dispersed.

Each recipe specifies an exact tracing time. When I tested the recipes, the temperature inside my kitchen ranged from 70 to 75 degrees F at 110 feet above sea level. If your kitchen is a much different altitude or temperature, it could shorten or extend the time soap takes to thicken. It's important to recognize tracing rather than depend on the exact time stated in a recipe.

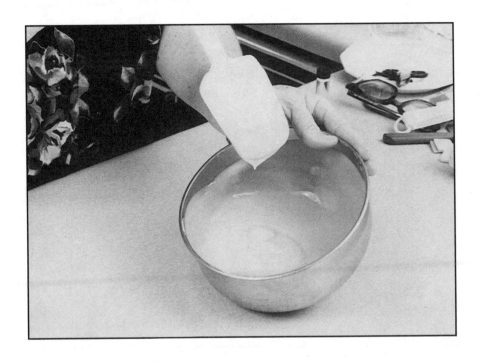

Drip some soap onto the surface of the soap in the bowl. It should leave a "trace" or a small mound.

Draw a line in the soap with a rubber spatula. If a "trace"
of the line remains after a few seconds, the soap has "traced."

Don't worry!

Tracing is easy to recognize, yet it causes new soapmakers more worry than any other aspect of soapmaking. (I know. I've done my share of worrying!) If the soap doesn't trace by the time specified in the recipe—relax and know that you have a good recipe. The soap you're making *will* trace eventually.

Stir crazy

When fat and lye combine to form soap, the soap has a tendency to sit at the bottom of the container and fat rises to the top of the soap. Stirring makes an even mixture.

While learning to make soap, I stirred it constantly until it traced. I even asked my son to stir it for me while I went to the bathroom! You can imagine the freedom I gained when I learned I didn't have to stir constantly.

Stirring does not cause soap to trace. A chemical reaction causes it; time and temperature are also important factors. The tracing times for these recipes range from a few minutes to hours. You don't have to stir the soap constantly.

- For soap with a tracing time of thirty minutes or longer, stir the soap for the first ten minutes after pouring in the lye; then every fifteen minutes until it traces.
- For soap with a tracing time of fifteen minutes or less, stir it constantly.

You forgot to stir the soap?

If you forget to stir soap that takes a long time to trace (an hour or more) chances are there's no problem. The mixture is still thin and you can stir it easily. If you forget to stir the soap and come back to a really thick mixture, one that is too thick to pour into the molds—that's a problem. Put the soap in a 200-degree oven for a few minutes. Higher temperatures can make soap more fluid. The soap thickens quickly as it cools. Take it from the oven, straight to the molds and quickly pour it into molds.

Hot stuff

Some recipes direct you to put the soap in a 200-degree oven as part of the tracing time. High temperatures speed saponification and make a harder bar of soap. The oven method is used only for soap that would otherwise take days to trace. Use pot holders or oven mitts to protect your hands from the heat.

Step 6. Add the fragrant oil and stir.

- For recipes with a tracing time longer than five minutes, add the fragrant oil during the last five minutes of the tracing time specified in the recipe.
- For recipes with a tracing time shorter than five minutes, add the fragrant oil immediately after you add the lye-water to the fat.

Step 7. Pour the soap into molds and wait the time specified as "time in molds" in the recipe.

Pour the soap into molds and use a rubber spatula to scrape the bowl clean. If necessary, gently tap the mold to level the soap.

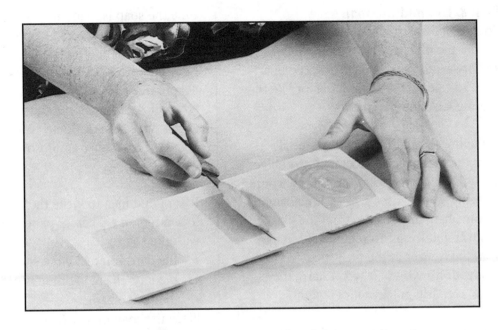

Overfill the molds slightly. After twenty-four hours, or when the soap hardens, use a knife to level the soap with the mold. Use the excess soap to make Confetti Soap (page 80) or Washballs (page 165).

Step 8. Unmold the soap

Soap is still harsh when it's time to remove it from the molds. Put on rubber gloves and press the back of each mold compartment to release the soap. It's a lot like removing ice cubes from a tray.

Sometimes soap doesn't release easily from the mold. To overcome this problem, leave the soap in a freezer for a few hours. Freezing soap causes it to contract slightly, become hard and release from the plastic mold. If you forget to remove the soap from the freezer at the time specified in the recipe, don't worry. It won't harm the soap, even if you leave it overnight.

Step 9: Wait the time specified in the recipe for the soap to "age."

To a soapmaker, the terms aging, curing and texturing-out refer to the time between pouring soap into molds and the time the soap is ready for use. The soap-making process doesn't stop when you pour the soap into molds. Over time, the lye continues to react with the fats, water evaporates and the bars harden. I call it "the aging process" and it usually takes about three weeks. Some types of soap benefit from longer aging so the bars become harder.

It's a good idea to write the following information on a piece of paper and place it with the soap:
• the date you make the soap
• the date the aging time is over
• the recipe name

Place the soap on plastic or cardboard and place it where it won't be disturbed. Turn the soap a few times during the aging period to expose all surfaces to air.

Step 10. Enjoy your soap!

As soap ages, a fine, white powder may appear on the surface. This is soda ash (calcium carbonate) formed by a reaction of lye with carbon dioxide in air. The white powder is mostly on the surface exposed to air while the soap was in molds. Soap that contains wax develops little or no soda ash. There are three ways to deal with soda ash:

- Try to prevent it

Immediately after pouring soap into molds, cover the soap with plastic wrap or waxed paper. Press the wrap or paper onto the surface of the soap to prevent air contact.

- Cut it away

Overfill the molds slightly. Later (when the soap hardens) take a knife and cut the soap level with the mold. This also cuts away the soda ash.

- Wash it away

Wait until the soap ages and wash the powder away by rubbing the soap with your hands under running water or by rubbing the soap over a wet dishcloth.

Clean up

After my first batch of soap, I figured that I could run hot water into the bowl and get lots of bubbles to clean everything. I was wrong. At this point the mixing bowl contains more fat than soap. Add soap or detergent to wash everything and place it in the dishwasher for further cleaning.

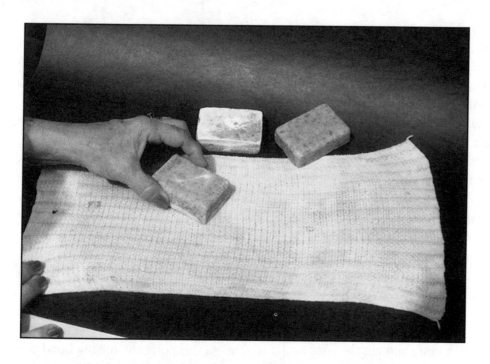

To remove stubborn white areas, rub the soap over a wet cloth.
When the soap is smooth and a uniform color, set it aside to dry.

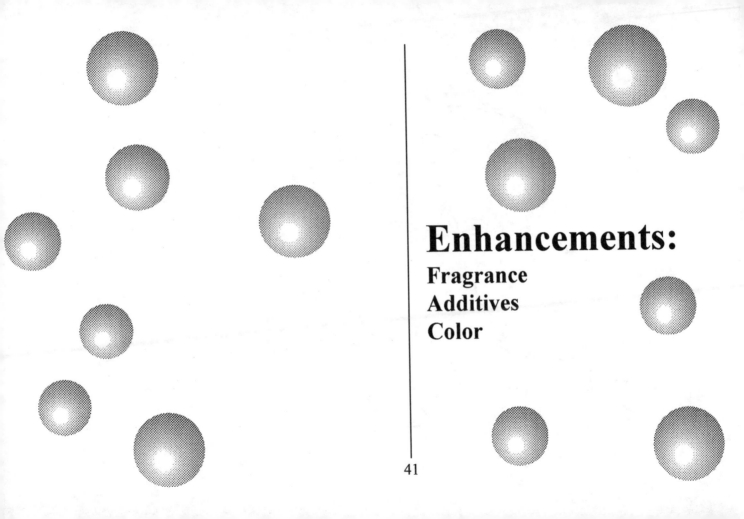

Enhancements:
Fragrance
Additives
Color

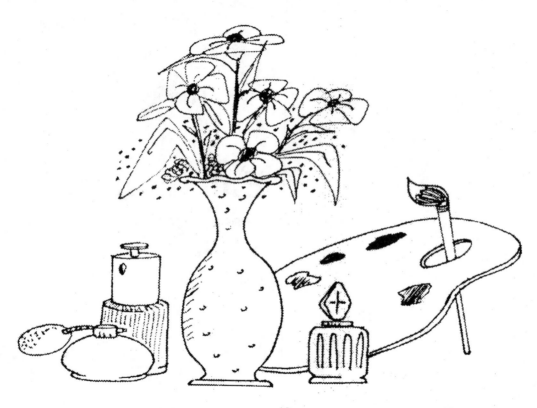

Fragrance

The addition of fragrant oils can lend variety to a soap recipe. It can also increase the chance of failure.

Watch for alcohol!

If a product contains alcohol, the label usually lists it as an ingredient (but not always). Add enough alcohol to soap and it can cause a separation of ingredients that no amount of stirring can remedy. Toilet water, cologne, after shave, tinctures and extracts smell great, but they contain a substantial amount of alcohol. Do not add them to soap. Most perfumes contain a lot of alcohol, but you can safely add perfume *oils* to soap.

Essential oils

Essential oils are extracted aromatic chemical compounds. "Chemical" is a key word here. Most essential oils have an acid pH, which can upset the chemical reaction of the lye and fats. A small amount of essential oil (about two teaspoons per pound of fat) is usually safe to add.

Concrete or absolute oils

Concrete or absolute oils are extracted with solvent. The solvent is removed, leaving only oil (similar to essential oil).

Perfume oils

If a product label states that the product can be used as perfume, then it can be added to soap. Such products are usually essential oils extended (weakened) by the addition of fixed oil. The fixed oil may not be listed on the label as an ingredient.

The amount of oil to use depends on the strength of the fragrance. Don't add more than one tablespoon of these lightly scented oils. The extra oil can throw off the lye-fat ratio of the soap recipe.

Natural-flavor oils

Natural-flavor oils add color, taste and aroma to food. You can add them to soap, but the fragrance is often lost. Some natural-flavor oils are food-safe essential oils with a stable fragrance: clove, cinnamon, spearmint and peppermint.

Other fragrances

Beware of potpourri oils and synthetic oils such as candle scents. If a label says "avoid skin contact" or "this oil may damage wood finishes," don't add it to soap. Most potpourri oils and stove-top simmering scents are candle scents that carry such warnings. If a label warns you that the product should not be used as perfume, then don't add it to soap.

Altered fragrances

Don't be alarmed by the strange scents that can come from the stirring bowl. Additives such as milk and starch can create some disagreeable scents that disappear as the soap ages. Lye and fat can react with fragrant oils and alter the resulting fragrance. Some fragrances disappear. Don't judge soap fragrance until the soap ages at least three weeks. A true test of soap fragrance is to judge it after three months.

Clean scents

Since lye and fat can alter the fragrance of some oils, it's difficult to make soap that smells just like strawberries or magnolias. It's best to strive for fresh, clean scents that cover the aroma of fat and lye. Some fragrant oils are more stable in soap than others. Stable scents include those listed in Appendix C, page 187.

Take no chances!

Because of their chemical structure, some essential oils cause problems in soap. Based on my tests, oils that cause problems are pine, anise and citrus oils (lemon, orange, and grapefruit). Take no chances with the fragrance you add to soap. Each recipe specifically names the type of fragrant oil successfully used in the test: either Lorann Oil® or oil from Sunfeather Herbal Soap Company™. If you choose to add other fragrances, you're in uncharted territory. The fragrance you substitute might work—it might not.

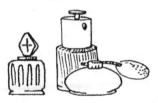

You may substitute the fragrant oils from one recipe to another. Just remember, if you exchange oils, it's no longer a tested recipe. The tracing time may be different from that stated in the recipe.

Additives

Additives are not required to make soap, but they can contribute some desirable characteristics.

Starch
Starches are grain cereals such as oatmeal, barley and rice flakes. These are not saponified and remain, more or less, in their true form in the finished soap. Starches are soothing to skin; they contribute texture to soap, and they can shorten the tracing time. You may omit starches from the recipes, but the soap may take longer to trace.

Milk
Milk contains casein that thickens the soap mixture and adds texture to the finished soap. You can use water instead of milk listed in the recipes, but the soap may take longer to trace.

Earth products
Pumice, fuller's earth, kaolin, bentonite and talc are not saponified and remain in their true form in soap. They contribute texture, make soap more opaque and thicken the soap mixture. You may omit them from any recipe, but expect a longer tracing time.

Wax
Wax in soap recipes shortens the tracing time, reduces the formation of soda ash and makes a harder bar of soap. If wax is listed in a recipe, then add it. It drastically affects the tracing time. Add waxes to the fats and apply medium heat until the wax melts. Don't attempt to melt the wax with

out the fats and never use high heat in an attempt to shorten the melting time. High temperatures present a fire hazard.

Petroleum products
You may omit petroleum products such as baby oil and mineral oil without affecting the tracing time. You may omit petroleum jelly, but the tracing time could increase.

Rosin (pine resin)
Rosin contributes hardness and a brown color to soap. It also shortens the tracing time. Rosin isn't necessary for saponification, but since it drastically affects the character of the soap, never omit it from a recipe.

Herbs
Herbs are optional ingredients. If used, they should be in powder form to avoid unnecessary abrasiveness in the finished soap. Herbs can thicken the soap mixture and shorten the tracing time. If you omit herbs from a recipe, expect the tracing time to increase slightly or it could remain the same.

Fruits and vegetables
Fresh fruits and vegetables rot, even when encased in soap. Most fruits are acid and can upset the ratio of lye to fat in the recipe. Vegetables can be added to soap if they are first, dried and then, ground to a fine powder.

Color it beautiful

I like natural soap.
After many years of soapmaking, I've become a soap purist. I seldom color soap and enjoy the natural colors which range from snow white to caramel tan, depending on the ingredients.

You want color?

Okay, but soap coloring must meet two requirements: it must be stable and it must be color-fast.

- Stable (stability)

Soap color must withstand the alkalinity of lye so that the color remains true (even after the soap ages).

- Color-fast

Color-fast means the soap keeps its color (without fading) and that the color doesn't come off the soap onto other surfaces. No matter what color the soap, the lather should be white. Colored lather may stain your hands. It will definitely stain washcloths and soap dishes.

Fruit juice, vegetable juice and natural plant dye

Fruit juice, vegetable juice and natural plant dye are not stable or color-fast.

Besides not providing the color you want, some juices alter the pH of the soap mixture and cause failure. (See page 185 for more about pH.)

Lake colors

Lake colors are used to color foods, drugs and cosmetics (FD & C). For instance, the ingredients of black food coloring are: FD & C Blue 2 Lake, FD & C Red 40 Lake and FD & C Yellow 6 Lake. Lake colors are sold in liquid, paste and powder form. I tested lake coloring powders and found that most of them are not stable in soap and that *none* of them are color-fast. (See Appendix F, page 190, for test results.) Lake colors are not suitable for adding color to soap.

What DOES work!

Pourette Candle Company® sells powdered aniline candle dye as soap color. It works well. It's stable, color-fast and very concentrated.

How to use Pourette's® powdered soap coloring

Add about 1/8 teaspoon color to a soap recipe for a light shade or add about 1/4 teaspoon for a medium-to-dark shade. Measure the amount of color desired and put it in a small, glass container. Follow the recipe and add the lye-water to the fats. Take about 1/4 teaspoon of the soap mixture and blend it with the coloring powder. Press any grains of color that remain whole and mix them thoroughly. Add a bit more soap, mix well and add the coloring to the main batch of soap.

Pourette® sells four soap colors: red, yellow, blue and green. Appendix D, page 188, shows how to combine the four colors and create many other colors. You may add or delete soap coloring in the recipes and it shouldn't affect the tracing time.

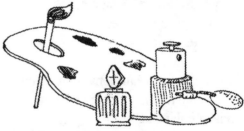

Matching colors and fragrances

The concept of matching colors and fragrances is worth mentioning. Here are some ideas.
- Match the color to the type fat:
    - yellow - sunflower oil
    - green - olive oil
    - white - almond oil

- Match the color to the name:
    black - Midnight soap
    deep blue - Blue Serenity
    red and yellow - Sunburst Blast

- Match the color to the type of filler:
    yellow-green - lemon balm
    light purple - lavender
    white - talc

- Green promotes harmony, contentment and stability. It is cooling and emotionally balancing.

- Yellow is warming and mentally stimulating.

- Violet promotes peace, love and inner balance. It aids concentration, mediation and prayer.

- Orange is energizing and warming. It instills excitement, confidence and joy.

- Blue is relaxing and cooling. It eases tension and relieves anxiety.

- Red increases warmth, energy and vitality. It demands attention and counteracts exhaustion.

- Magenta is formal, festive and forceful. It stimulates affection.

- Turquoise is calming. It eases tension, reduces fatigue and relieves anxiety.

The Recipes

The Recipes

By now you should be experiencing a soapmaking adrenaline rush. For the infinitely curious, it's the moment you've been waiting for—the recipes! Follow the directions outlined on page 29 to make any kind of soap.

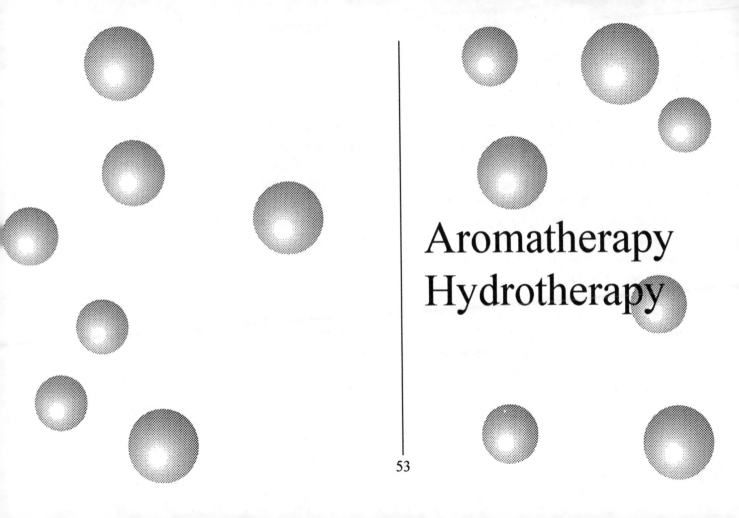

Aromatherapy
Hydrotherapy

Aromatherapy and Hydrotherapy

These recipes are designed for more than just clean skin. Hydrotherapy is the treatment of body ailments with water (notably baths). Aromatherapy is the use of fragrances to benefit physical, mental, and spiritual well being. It has been practiced since ancient times. A few scientific studies seem to substantiate beneficial qualities of aromatherapy.

Aromatherapists believe that people with epilepsy should avoid sweet fennel, hyssop, sage and rosemary. They believe that people with high blood pressure should avoid hyssop, rosemary, sage and thyme.

Aromatherapists further advise that pregnant women should avoid bitter almond, basil, clary sage, clove bud, hyssop, sweet fennel, juniper berry, marjoram, myrrh, peppermint, rose, rosemary, sage, pennyroyal, thyme and wintergreen essential oils.

Zzzzzzzzzzzzzzz

(For restful sleep)

Why not slip into the comfort and warmth of a bath designed to create a relaxing atmosphere? Catch up on your *z*'s with these yawn-inducing herbs. The lingering floral scent is sure to promote sweet dreams.

5 ounces coconut oil
5 ounces olive oil
3 ounces cocoa butter
3 ounces safflower oil
1/2 ounce beeswax

2.5 ounces lye
1 cup cold water

Optional ingredients:
1 teaspoon baby oatmeal (dry)
1 teaspoon chamomile blossoms
1 teaspoon hops
1 teaspoon lemon balm
1 teaspoon marjoram
1 teaspoon valerian

Fragrance:
1 1/2 teaspoons lavender oil
1/2 teaspoon neroli perfume oil
1/2 teaspoon ylang-ylang oil
1/4 teaspoon sandalwood oil

Fat temperature: 160 degrees F
Lye-water temperature: 140 degrees F
Tracing time: 3 minutes
Time in molds: 24 hours
Place the soap in a freezer for 3 hours, then remove it from the molds.
Age: 6 weeks

Hippocrates Healer
(For healing)

Hippocrates believed that bathing is an invaluable means of preserving health. Why not try his prescription for whatever ails your mind, body or spirit? Don't think about it—just say, "Yes!" and add water.

8 ounces cocoa butter
8 ounces olive oil

2.2 ounces lye
3/4 cup cold water

Optional ingredients:
1 teaspoon calendula petals
1 teaspoon chamomile

(Optional ingredients continued)
1 teaspoon marjoram
1 teaspoon thyme
1/8 teaspoon grape soap color
(prepared by the chart on page 188)

Fragrance:
2 teaspoons lavender oil
1/4 teaspoon natural clove oil (leaf)

Fat temperature: 105 degrees F
Lye-water temperature: 155 degrees F
Tracing time: 10 minutes
Time in molds: 24 hours
Age: 3 weeks

> Vincent Priessntz is called
> the father of medicinal bathing,
> or hydrotherapy.

Therapeutic Bath

(For stress, muscle aches and congestion)

Relax and say "aaah" as Therapeutic Mustard Bath jump-starts your circulation, opens pores and relieves stress. Use this soap with hot water to soothe muscle aches and relieve congestion. I promise you'll feel alive and invigorated.

14 ounces lard
2 ounces coconut oil

2.4 ounces lye
1/2 cup cold water

Optional ingredients:
2 tablespoons mustard powder

(Optional ingredients continued)
1/8 teaspoon Pourette® blue soap color

Fragrance:
1/2 teaspoon eucalyptus oil
1/2 teaspoon rosemary oil
1/2 teaspoon wintergreen oil
1/16 teaspoon thyme oil

Fat temperature: 90 degrees F
Lye-water temperature: 155 degrees F
Tracing time: 3 minutes
Time in molds: 24 hours
Age: 3 weeks

> A built-in bathtub and drainage system more than 3,000 years old lies in the ruins of King Nestor's palace near Pylos, Greece.

Thyme Out
(To combat fatigue)

To comfort a tired mind and body, nothing can beat the triple treat of thyme, lavender and rosemary. This soap works as hard as you do to combat the stress of a long, hard day. If your skin is normal or oily, add about 1/4 cup sea salt to the bath water and take Thyme Out to soak those aches and pains away.

6 ounces coconut oil
3 ounces avocado oil
3 ounces olive oil
3 ounces shortening
1 ounce cocoa butter
1/2 ounce beeswax

2.5 ounce lye
1 cup cold water

Optional ingredients:
1 tablespoon mint
1 tablespoon rosemary
1 teaspoon thyme
1/16 teaspoon Pourette® red soap color

Fragrance:
1 teaspoon rosemary oil
1/4 teaspoon peppermint oil
1/16 teaspoon thyme oil

Fat temperature: 150 degrees F
Lye-water temperature: 150 degrees F
Tracing time: 20 minutes
Time in molds: 24 hours
Place the soap in a freezer for 3 hours, then remove it from the molds.
Age: 4 weeks

Peppermint Flip
(For increased energy)

There's no doubt about it—cool baths refresh. In fact, they are so stimulating, you should limit them to five or ten minutes. When a cool touch is in order, Peppermint Flip is instant energy for those times you really need it. If this sounds too good to be true, maybe you should check it out for yourself!

7 ounces coconut oil
7 ounces olive oil
2 ounces cocoa butter
1/2 ounce beeswax

2.5 ounces lye
1 cup cold water

Optional ingredients:
1 tablespoon rosemary
1 teaspoon rosin (pine resin)
1/8 teaspoon cinnamon
1/8 teaspoon Pourette® red soap color

Fragrance:
1 1/2 teaspoons peppermint oil
1/2 teaspoon cinnamon oil
1/4 teaspoon rosemary oil
1/8 teaspoon lemon grass oil

Fat temperature: 145 degrees F
Lye-water temperature: 150 degrees F
Tracing time: 5 minutes
Time in molds: 24 hours
Place the soap in a freezer for 3 hours, then remove it from the molds.
Age: 4 weeks

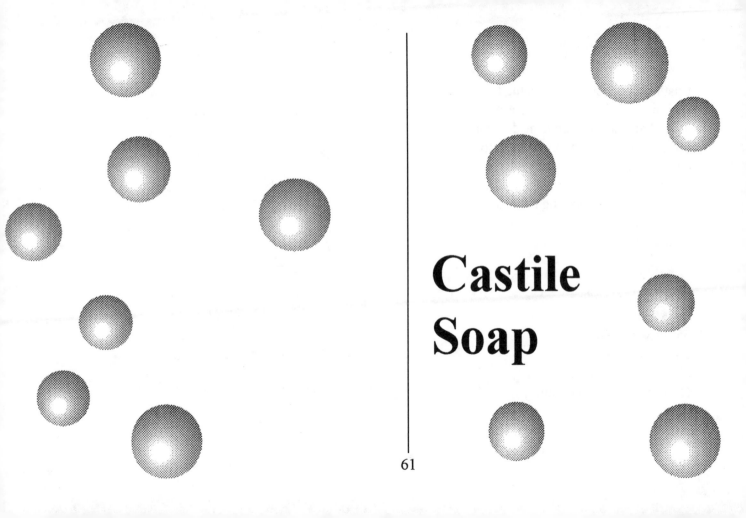

Castile
Soap

Castile Soap

Castile soap is named from the Castila region of Spain where olives are abundant. True castile soap is made from 100% olive oil. If you're lucky enough to find castile soap in stores today, chances are it's with beauty products, not with bath soap. With the following recipes, you can create classic castile soap from bygone days.

Castile soap is a great shampoo bar!

Classic Castile

Go for the magic of Classic Castile soap: better mildness—better soap— better check it out!

16 ounces olive oil

2.2 ounces lye
3/4 cup cold water

Optional ingredient:
1/4 teaspoon Pourette® blue soap color

Fragrance:
1 teaspoon lavender oil
1/4 teaspoon artificial bergamot oil
1/4 teaspoon jasmine perfume oil

Fat temperature: 150 degrees F
Lye-water temperature: 150 degrees F
Tracing time: 2 days
Time in molds: 6 days
Age: 8 weeks

Add the lye-water to the fat. Stir constantly for the first 10 minutes and often during the first hour. Leave the soap in the stirring bowl for two days. Stir the soap occasionally. Stir in the fragrant oil, pour the soap into molds and leave it six days. Place the soap in a freezer for twelve hours, then remove it from the molds; age eight weeks.

> A warm bath (98 to 102 degrees F) for thirty minutes to one hour promotes relaxation and restful sleep.

Castile Soap

Morning Glory

All the right ingredients come together for everything you've always wanted in a soap—an all-in-one bath soap and shampoo! (See page 157.) You should definitely add this soap to your personal collection.

14 ounces olive oil
2 ounces cocoa butter
1/2 ounce beeswax

2.2 ounces lye
1 cup cold water

Optional ingredient:
1 tablespoon henna
1/8 teaspoon Pourette® yellow soap color

Fragrance:
2 teaspoons neroli perfume oil
1 teaspoon sandalwood oil
1/8 teaspoon natural clove oil (leaf)

Fat temperature: 140 degrees F
Lye-water temperature: 150 degrees F
Tracing time: 30 minutes
Time in molds: 2 days
Place the soap in a freezer over night, then remove it from the molds.
Age: 4 weeks

After-bath Splash
(for oily or normal skin)

Combine two cups rose water and one cup vodka (any proof). Splash the mixture over clean skin to close skin pores and to make your skin feel fresh and smooth.

Castile Soap

Private Retreat

Private Retreat leaves you refreshed and renewed with a sense of physical and emotional well-being. Indulge yourself often! (See page 157 for shampoo.)

8 ounces coconut oil
8 ounces olive oil
1/4 ounce beeswax

2.6 ounces lye
3/4 cup cold water

Optional ingredients:
1 tablespoon henna
1 tablespoon rosemary
1/8 teaspoon Pourette® blue soap color

Fragrance:
1 teaspoon rosemary oil
1/8 teaspoon lemon grass oil

Fat temperature: 160 degrees F
Lye-water temperature: 150 degrees F
Tracing time: 1 hour, 30 minutes
Time in molds: 24 hours
Place the soap in a freezer for 3 hours, then remove it from the molds.
Age: 4 weeks

Soap Sponge
To make a sudsy scrubber
for bathing, slit a sponge and insert
small bits of soap.

Castile Soap

Rain Perfume

Surrender to the spell of Sunfeather Herbal Soap Company's™ Rain Perfume Oil. Rain Perfume creates an aura of freshness to awaken your spirit. You owe it to yourself to experience this Rolls-Royce of soap fragrances.

12 ounces olive oil
4 ounces palm oil

2.3 ounces lye
1 cup cold water

Fragrance:
1 1/2 teaspoons Sunfeather™
Rain Perfume Oil

Fat temperature: 100 degrees F
Lye-water temperature: 125 degrees F
Tracing time: 3 hours
Time in molds: 24 hours
Place the soap in a freezer for 3 hours, then remove it from the molds.
Age: 3 weeks

Beeswax Castile

Beeswax speeds the tracing time of olive oil to an amazing twelve minutes! If you are in a hurry to experience the luxury of castile soap, this is the recipe for you— all the ingredients needed for a soothing and sensual bath.

13 ounces olive oil
2 ounces beeswax
1 ounce palm oil

2.1 ounce lye
1 cup cold water

Fragrance:
1 teaspoon artificial bergamot oil
1 teaspoon sassafras oil

(Fragrance continued)
1/2 teaspoon jasmine perfume oil
1/4 teaspoon natural clove oil (leaf)

Fat temperature: 160 degrees F
Lye-water temperature: 150 degrees F
Tracing time: 12 minutes
Time in molds: 24 hours
Place the soap in a freezer for 3 hours, then remove it from the molds.
Age: 6 weeks

"Hy-droh-jen-AY-shun"
Hydrogenation is a chemical process that adds hydrogen to a substance. Liquid fats are often hydrogenated to solidify them and to improve their odor and flavor.
Shortening is hydrogenated fat.

Lightly Lemon Castile

From the early 1900s until today, many soapmakers call the soap they produce "castile" even though it contains many fats other than olive. Lemon provides a fresh-as-the-morning fragrance to this castile-imitator.

8 ounces olive oil
4 ounces beef tallow
4 ounces coconut oil

2.4 ounces lye
3/4 cup cold water

Optional ingredient:
1/4 teaspoon Pourette® yellow soap color

Fragrance:
1 1/2 teaspoons lemon grass oil
1/2 teaspoon artificial bergamot oil
1/4 teaspoon patchouli oil

Fat temperature: 120 degrees F
Lye-water temperature: 160 degrees F
Tracing time: 2 hours
Time in molds: 3 days
Place the soap in a freezer for 3 hours, then remove it from the molds.
Age: 6 weeks

In 1826, English chemist
William Perkin produced
the first aniline dye.
He accidentally invented
a violet dye when he tried
to prepare quinine.

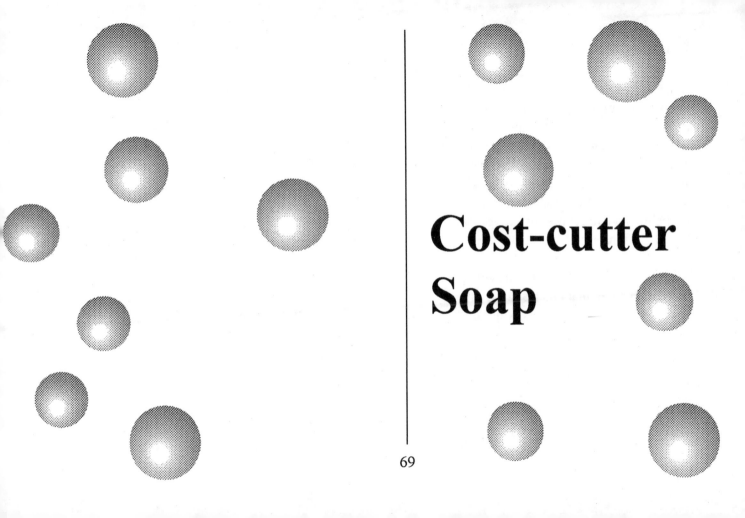

Cost-cutter
Soap

Cost-cutter Soap

Since animal fat is often discarded or sold for pennies a pound, this chapter is dedicated to people with a "waste not; want not" attitude. Grocery stores sell pork fat as lard and Sunfeather Soap Company sells beef tallow. If you want to make soap from the fat of other animals, you'll probably have to render the fat yourself. The directions are on page 189.

Soap from pork and beef fat provide the best lather of animal fats tested. Goat and sheep fat need the help of coconut oil for rich lather.

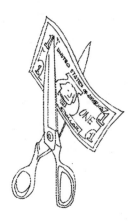

Divinely Bovine
(beef fat)

Soap from beef fat is creamy white and it produces great lather, even without coconut oil.

16 ounces beef tallow
2.3 ounces lye
3/4 cup cold water

Optional fragrance:
1 tablespoon essential oil

Fat temperature: 120 degrees F
Lye-water temperature: 155 degrees F
Tracing time: 2 minutes
Time in molds: 24 hours
Age: 3 weeks

Ivory Splendor
(pork fat)

Soap from pork fat also produces great lather without the addition of coconut oil. For an even mixture, stir this soap with a whisk instead of a rubber spatula.

16 ounces lard

2.3 ounces lye
1/2 cup cold water

Optional fragrance:
1 tablespoon essential oil

Fat temperature: 90 degrees F
Lye-water temperature: 155 degrees F
Tracing time: 5 minutes
Time in molds: 24 hours
Age: 3 weeks

Supremely Caprine
(goat fat)

I don't have much to say in defense of
soap made from goat fat. It is very hard
and doesn't produce much lather. It's best
to use the "improved" recipe.

16 ounces goat fat
2.5 ounces lye
1/2 cup water
Optional fragrance:
1 tablespoon essential oil
Fat temperature: 80 degrees F
Lye-water temperature: 170 degrees F
Tracing time: 35 minutes
Time in molds: 24 hours
Age: 3 weeks

Soap from goat fat— Improved!

The combination of coconut oil and goat
fat makes soap far superior to soap made
from goat fat alone.

10 ounces goat fat
6 ounces coconut oil
2.7 ounces lye
1/2 cup water
Optional fragrance:
1 tablespoon essential oil
Fat temperature: 145 degrees F
Lye-water temperature: 145 degrees F
Tracing time: 45 minutes
Time in molds: 24 hours
Age: 3 weeks

Marco Polo
(sheep fat)

Soap from sheep fat is snow white and very hard, but it doesn't lather very well. I recommend the "improved" recipe that follows this one.

16 ounces sheep fat
2.4 ounces lye
1/2 cup water
Optional fragrance:
1 tablespoon essential oil
Fat temperature: 100 degrees F
Lye-water temperature: 150 degrees F
Tracing time: 50 minutes
Time in molds: 24 hours
Age: 3 weeks

Soap from sheep fat—improved!

Soap from coconut oil and sheep fat lathers well, but it cracks! Olive oil solves the cracking problem and makes a beautifully smooth soap.

10 ounces sheep fat
4 ounces coconut oil
2 ounces olive oil
2.5 ounces lye
1/2 cup water
Optional fragrance:
1 tablespoon essential oil
Fat temperature: 155 degrees F
Lye-water temperature: 155 degrees F
Tracing time: 50 minutes
Time in molds: 24 hours
Age: 3 weeks

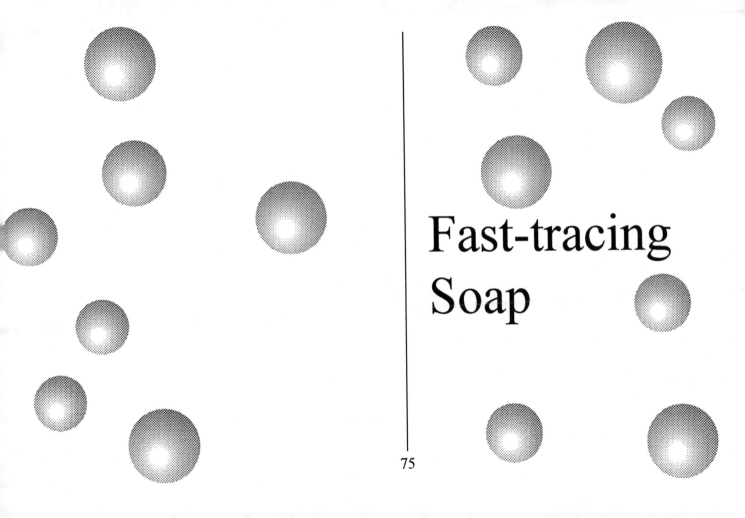

Fast-tracing
Soap

Fast-tracing Soap

"Cobble up" means to put together quickly and that's just what you do with the fast-tracing soap in this chapter. Can you spare ten minutes to make soap? Sure you can! Here is an eclectic mix of recipes that makes soapmaking a cinch.

The Bizarre Bar

Peruvian balsam makes this soap a beautiful brown color filled with darker-brown specks of balsam. The lather from this soap is quite unique. The best I can describe it is "silky." The warm, sensual vanilla fragrance satisfies the most seasoned soap epicurean.

10 ounces olive oil
4 ounces palm oil
1/2 ounce beeswax

2.0 ounces lye
1 cup cold water

Optional ingredient:
1/2 teaspoon Peruvian balsam

Fragrance:
1 teaspoon vanillin powder, USP

Fat temperature: 150 degrees F
Lye-water temperature: 140 degrees F
Add the lye-water to the fats and stir the soap with a wire whisk to break up the large lumps of balsam; small lumps can remain.
Tracing time: 15 minutes
Time in molds: 24 hours
Place the soap in a freezer for 3 hours, then remove it from the molds.
Age: 8 weeks

Soap and warm water
are your first line of defense
against germs: wash minor cuts,
burns, scrapes and blisters thoroughly.

Tickled Pink

This beautiful pink soap is sure to tickle your fancy and a spicy rose fragrance adds to the fun. Why not get in on the action of the first and only soap that entertains while it cleans!

7 ounces lard
7 ounces shortening
2 ounces coconut oil

2.3 ounces lye
3/4 cup cold water

Optional ingredient:
1/16 teaspoon Pourette® red soap color

Fragrance:
1 1/2 teaspoons bois de rose

(Fragrance continued)
1/2 teaspoon natural clove oil (leaf)

Fat temperature: 90 degrees F
Lye-water temperature: 150 degrees F
Tracing time: 10 minutes
Time in molds: 24 hours
Place the soap in a freezer for 3 hours, then remove it from the molds.
Age: 3 weeks

Proctor and Gamble's Ivory Soap® was first sold July, 1879 and advertised as 99 44/100% pure. It was named from the Bible's forty-fifth Psalm:

With myrrh and aloes and cassia
your robes are fragrant;
from ivory palaces
string music brings you joy.

Blue Lightning

If fast-tracing were a crime, this soap would definitely deserve a speeding ticket. The culprit responsible?—carnauba wax, a natural wax obtained from the leaves of Brazilian wax palms. The arresting lavender-rose fragrance definitely puts this soap on the most wanted list.

9 ounces shortening
4 ounces coconut oil
2 ounces sunflower oil
1 ounce carnauba wax

2.3 ounces lye
1 cup cold water

Optional ingredient:
1/4 teaspoon Pourette® blue soap color

Fragrance:
1 1/2 teaspoons bois de rose
1 1/2 teaspoons lavender oil
1/2 teaspoon neroli perfume oil

Fat temperature: 170 degrees F
Lye-water temperature: 130 degrees F
This soap traces quickly, but stir it constantly and scrape the sides of the bowl for eight minutes before you pour it into molds.
Tracing time: 8 minutes
Time in molds: 48 hours
Place the soap in a freezer for 12 hours, then remove it from the molds.
Age: 8 weeks

Festive Confetti Soap

Soap filled with soap! Confetti Soap is an elegant answer to the problem of soap scraps. To make it, make soap as you normally would and fill the molds. Scrape every last bit of soap from the mixing bowl into a "scrap container."

- Take small pieces of soap from the bath, chop them and add them to the scrap container.

- Squish small pieces of soft soap to form flat, round shapes and add them to the collection.

- If desired, plan color themes: black, orange and yellow for Halloween or red and green chips for Christmas.

When you collect about two cups of soap scraps, it's time for a soapmaking party!

(Festive Confetti Soap continued)

This recipe traces quickly (five minutes!) to form a basic white soap. It's a perfect background for colorful bits of soap.

8 ounces shortening
6 ounces lard
2 ounces coconut oil

2.3 ounces lye
1/2 cup cold water

Optional ingredient:
2 cups chopped soap

Fragrance:
1 1/2 teaspoons rosemary oil
1 1/2 teaspoons natural clove oil (leaf)

Fat temperature: 130 degrees F
Lye-water temperature: 175 degrees F
Tracing time: 5 minutes

Add the lye-water to the fats and stir for five minutes. Add the fragrant oils and soap scraps; stir well. When you pour this soap into molds, don't worry about pieces of soap sticking out of the mold at all angles. When the soap hardens, take a knife and cut the soap level with the mold.
Time in mold: 24 hours
Place the soap in a freezer for 3 hours, then remove it from the molds.
Age: 3 weeks

Herbal Heyday

After a long march, the Romans added rosemary to baths to relieve tired limbs. In ancient times, sage was the symbol of wisdom; thus wise ones are called "sages." You'll be equally wise to relax in a warm bath with this soap after a long, hard day.

7 ounces olive oil
6 ounces coconut oil
3 ounces cocoa butter
1 ounce beeswax

2.6 ounces lye
1 cup cold water

Optional ingredients:
1 tablespoon chamomile
1 teaspoon rosemary
1 teaspoon sage
1/8 teaspoon turquoise soap color

Fragrance:
1 teaspoon rosemary oil
1/2 teaspoon bois de rose.

Fat temperature: 150 degrees F
Lye-water temperature: 145 degrees F
Tracing time: 5 minutes
Time in molds: 24 hours
Place the soap in a freezer for 3 hours, then remove it from the molds.
Age: 3 weeks

Emperor Charlemagne held court while relaxing in a warm bath.

Fast-tracing Soap

Monograms and Designs

This white soap traces quickly. It's a good background for colored monograms and designs. (See page 159.)

8 ounces lard
6 ounces shortening
2 ounces coconut oil

2.3 ounces lye
1/2 cup cold water

Fragrance:
1 1/2 teaspoons natural clove oil (leaf)
1 1/2 teaspoons lemon grass oil
1 1/2 teaspoons rosemary oil

Fat temperature: 120 degrees F
Lye-water temperature: 175 degrees F
Tracing time: 15 minutes
Time in molds: 24 hours
Age: 3 weeks

Instant Creativity

In my creative efforts, I sometimes go over the edge. This soap is inspired by none other than walnut oil, a specialty salad oil. The gentle essence of lemon grass provides a clean scent prized in bath soaps. As far as color and fillers are concerned—enjoy the spectrum of choice!

6 ounces coconut oil
6 ounces shortening
4 ounces walnut oil

2.5 ounces lye
1/2 cup cold water

Optional ingredients:
1 teaspoon chamomile

(Optional ingredients continued)
1 teaspoon lavender
1 teaspoon lemon balm
1 teaspoon marjoram
1 teaspoon nuts (any kind, pressed and ground to form a paste-like consistency)
1 teaspoon sage
soap color as desired

Fragrance:
1 1/2 teaspoons artificial bergamot oil
1/4 teaspoon lemon grass oil

Fat temperature: 125 degrees F
Lye-water temperature: 160 degrees F
Tracing time: 5 minutes
Time in molds: 24 hours
Age: 3 weeks

Note: This soap traces instantly. Add the fragrant oils, stir five minutes and pour the soap into molds.

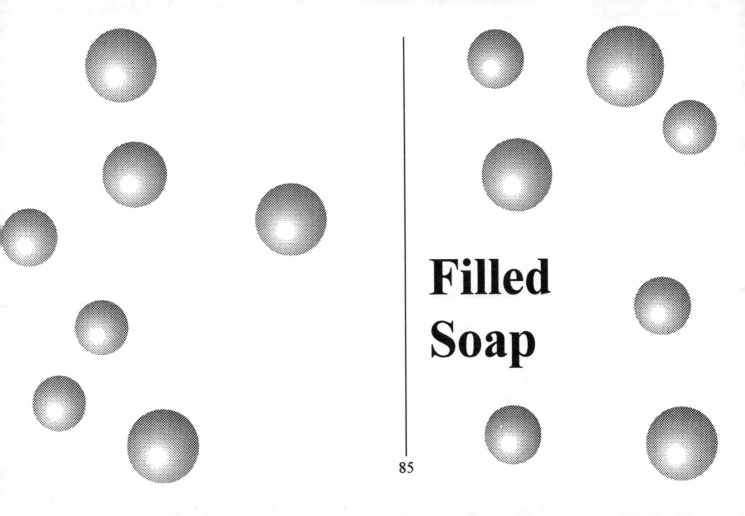

Filled
Soap

Filled Soap

In the late 1800s, soap manufacturers often added fillers such as clay, rosin (pine resin) and talc to soap. Fillers added bulk to soap, they were inexpensive and they increased manufacturers' profits. The best soap of 1897 was thought to be pure soap with no fillers. Today's soapmaker at home not only adds the fillers already mentioned, but oatmeal, cornmeal and many others.

I like filled soap. Fillers such as almond meal, oatmeal and cornmeal contain starches, which are soothing to the skin. The fillers in these recipes are optional ingredients which can be omitted or added to other recipes.

87 Purple Mountain Majesty
88 Mother Earth
89 Almond-oatmeal Soap
90 The Mean, Green Washing Machine
91 Soap Stones
92 Creature Comfort
93 Nude Interlude
94 German Yellow Soap

Filled Soap

Purple Mountain Majesty

Don't let the simplicity of this recipe fool you. The soap is very hard, produces great lather and has a sweet, floral fragrance. Soap doesn't get much better than this.

8 ounces beef tallow
4 ounces coconut oil
4 ounces shortening

2.4 ounces lye
3/4 cup water

Optional ingredients:
1 tablespoon talc or baby powder
1/4 teaspoon grape soap color

Fragrance:
1/2 teaspoon jasmine perfume oil
1/2 teaspoon lavender oil
1/2 teaspoon rosemary oil

Fat temperature: 125 degrees F
Lye-water temperature: 160 degrees F
Tracing time: 40 minutes
Time in mold: 24 hours
Age: 3 weeks

In 1858, Hamilton E. Smith
of Philadelphia patented one of the first
mechanical washing machines.
By 1919, granulated laundry soap
was widely available:
Proctor & Gamble's Ivory Snow®
Lever Brothers' Rinso®
Colgate's Fab®

87

Filled Soap

Mother Earth

The best ingredients Mother Earth has to offer come together in this down-to-earth natural soap.

6 ounces sweet almond oil
4 ounces coconut oil
4 ounces shortening
2 ounces palm oil

2.4 ounces lye
1 cup cold water

Optional ingredients:
3 tablespoons fuller's earth
2 tablespoons rosin (pine resin)
1 tablespoon chamomile

Fragrance:
1 1/2 teaspoons artificial bergamot oil

Fat temperature: 180 degrees F
Lye-water temperature: 135 degrees F
Tracing time: 30 minutes
Time in molds: 24 hours
Place the soap in a freezer for 3 hours, then remove it from the molds.
Age: 6 weeks

If your skin is sensitive, choose an abrasive-free, superfatted soap. Limit baths to ten minutes in tepid or cool water. Lightly pat yourself dry (no rubbing), then apply a moisturizer to your damp skin.

Filled Soap

Almond-oatmeal Soap

The starch in baby oatmeal is a tender approach to softer skin. This doubly-good soap also contains almond paste, to gently stimulate skin. This creamy bath pleasure is guaranteed to give your bath a boost.

7 ounces shortening
5 ounces coconut oil
4 ounces sweet almond oil

2.4 ounces lye
3/4 cup cold water

Optional ingredients:
1/2 cup baby oatmeal (dry)
1 tablespoon old-fashioned, flaked oats

(Optional ingredients continued)
1 teaspoon almonds (pressed and ground to a paste-like consistency)

Fragrance:
1 teaspoon Peruvian balsam
1/16 teaspoon oil of bitter almonds

Fat temperature: 130 degrees F
Lye-water temperature: 150 degrees F
Tracing time: 1 hour
Time in molds: 24 hours
Place the soap in a freezer for 3 hours, then remove it from the molds.
Age: 4 weeks

Note: Please don't substitute instant or quick-cooking oats in this recipe. They create a slimy problem!

Filled Soap

The Mean, Green Washing Machine

Pumice is a stony substance from volcanoes that's lighter than water! Use it to remove grease and tough dirt from hands and underneath fingernails. This soap is definitely a mean, green washing machine.

6 ounces beef tallow
6 ounces lard
4 ounces coconut oil

2.5 ounces lye
1 cup cold water

Optional ingredients:
2 tablespoons 2F pumice

(Optional ingredients continued)
1 teaspoon cardamom
1 teaspoon coriander
1/8 teaspoon Pourette® green soap color

Fragrance:
1 1/2 teaspoon lemon grass oil

Fat temperature: 100 degrees F
Lye-water temperature: 160 degrees F
Tracing time: 45 minutes
Time in molds: 24 hours
Age: 3 weeks

In AD 217, the Roman baths
of Caracalla held 16,000 bathers
at one time.

Soap Stones

I'm not perfect. I'll admit that Soap Stones were invented when I added too much pumice to a soap recipe. To use Soap Stones, soak your feet in soapy water for about thirty minutes to soften them. (See page 164.) Wet a Soap Stone and rub it over calluses. Rough skin disappears, leaving your feet smooth and invigorated.

To make Soap Stones, choose a recipe with a tracing time of twenty minutes or longer. Add 1/2 cup 2F pumice to one cup liquid soap; stir well. Pour the mixture into molds. Age Soap Stones the time specified in the recipe.

"Shouldn't you make those Soap Stones a little smaller?"

Filled Soap

Creature Comfort

The creature to be comforted is you when you envelope yourself with lather from this basic soap with soothing rice starch.

8 ounces lard
4 ounces coconut oil
4 ounces olive oil

2.4 ounces lye
3/4 cup cold water

Optional ingredient:
1/2 cup baby rice cereal (dry)

Fragrance:
3/4 teaspoon lemon grass oil

(Fragrance continued)
1/2 teaspoon lavender oil
3/8 teaspoon caraway oil
1/4 teaspoon rosemary oil

Fat temperature: 90 degrees F
Lye-water temperature: 160 degrees F
Tracing time: 48 hours
Stir the soap as often as desired, but at least three times daily.
Time in molds: 48 hours
Place the soap in a freezer for 3 hours, then remove it from the molds.
Age: 4 weeks

In the United States, popular spas include those at Hot Springs, Arkansas; Colorado Springs, Colorado and Battle Creek, Michigan.

Filled Soap

Nude Interlude

The procedure to make this creamy milk soap deviates from the standard. Follow the directions on this page.

16 ounces lard

2.3 ounces lye
1/2 cup cold water

Optional ingredient:
1 cup cold milk (skim or 2% fat)

Fragrance:
3/4 teaspoon jasmine perfume oil
3/4 teaspoon lavender oil
1/2 teaspoon rosemary oil

Fat temperature: 80 degrees F
Lye-water temperature: 165 degrees F
Tracing time: 1 hour, 20 minutes
Time in molds: 24 hours
Put the soap in a freezer for 3 hours, then remove it from the molds.
Age: 4 weeks

Directions:
Heat the fat. Mix the lye into the cold water. When the fat and lye-water reach the specified temperatures, pour the lye-water into the fat and mix well. Add the milk (cold from the refrigerator) and stir with a whisk for ten minutes. Stir the mixture occasionally (about every fifteen minutes) until it traces (about one hour and twenty minutes). Pour the soap into molds and wait twenty-four hours. Put the soap in a freezer for three hours, then remove it from the molds.

Filled Soap

German Yellow Soap

I tailored this recipe from one in a soap manufacturer's manual dated 1881. You need to work quickly to combine the ingredients and beat the three-minute tracing time. No artificial coloring is necessary for this soap; the rosin makes it a natural, golden brown.

9 ounces coconut oil
4 ounces shortening
2 ounces cocoa butter
1 ounce rosin (pine resin)
1 ounce soybean oil

2.6 ounces lye
3/4 cup cold water

Fragrance:
1/2 teaspoon fir needle oil
1/2 teaspoon rosemary oil

Fat temperature: 100 degrees F
Lye-water temperature: 160 degrees F
Tracing time: 3 minutes
Add the lye-water to the fats, and immediately add the rosin and fragrance.
Time in molds: 24 hours
Place the soap in a freezer for 3 hours, then remove it from the molds.
Age: 3 weeks

> **Non-drying After-bath Splash**
> (for all skin types)
> Combine 1 1/2 cups rose water with 1 1/2 cups witch hazel liquid. Splash the mixture over clean skin to remove traces of soap and to close skin pores. Your skin will feel fresh, healthy and smooth.

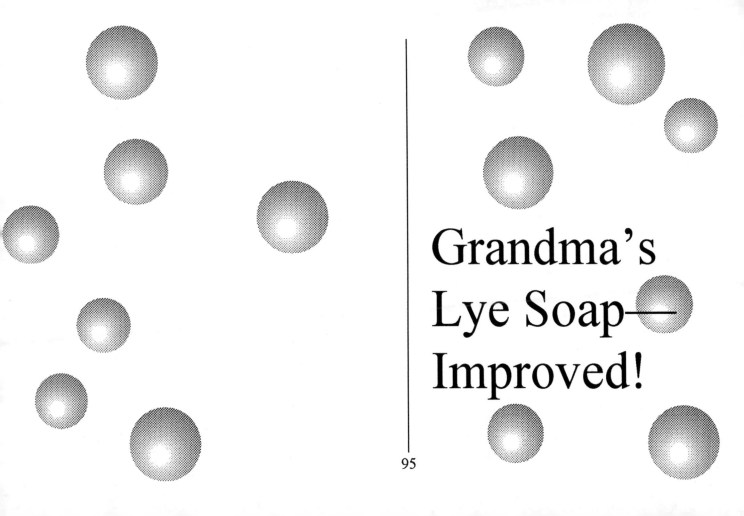

Grandma's Lye Soap— Improved!

Grandma's Lye Soap—Improved!

Our great-grandparents made soap from fat and home-made lye. The fats they used were usually lard and beef tallow. Soap made from these fats clean as well as any soap. Coconut oil increases the lather of soap made from animal fat. This is real soap, guaranteed to take you back to a simpler time. Also see Cost-cutter Soap (page 69) and how to render animal fat (page 189).

Grandma's Lye Soap—Improved!

Hive Robber

If our great-grandparents had known how much beeswax improves lard soap, they would have robbed the bee hive before making every batch. The light fragrance suits man, woman and beast.

15 ounces lard
1/2 ounce beeswax

2.2 ounces lye
3/4 cup cold water

Fragrance:
1 1/2 teaspoon spike oil (tech)
1/4 teaspoon lavender oil
1/4 teaspoon rosemary oil

(Fragrance continued)
1/8 teaspoon natural clove oil (leaf)

Fat temperature: 170 degrees F
Lye-water temperature: 150 degrees F
Tracing time: 12 minutes
Time in molds: 24 hours
Place the soap in a freezer for 3 hours, then remove it from the molds.
Age: 4 weeks

Soap Box
A box, especially a wooden box, in which soap is packed; an empty wooden box of this kind used as a temporary platform by speakers; characteristic of impassioned orators.

Grandma's Lye Soap—Improved!

Camphorated Soap

Our great-grandparents considered camphorated soap essential to clean cuts, scratches and rashes. Camphor produces a pleasant, cooling effect. If you have a cold, bathe with this soap. Making it definitely cleared my sinuses!

8 ounces beef tallow
8 ounces coconut oil

2.6 ounces lye
3/4 cup cold water

Optional ingredient:
1/8 teaspoon Pourette® blue soap color

Fragrance:
1 tablespoon camphor oil
1/4 teaspoon rosemary oil

Fat temperature: 100 degrees F
Lye-water temperature: 170 degrees F
Tracing time: 35 minutes
Time in molds: 24 hours
Age: 3 weeks

In Michigan, Dr. John H. Kellogg
served as the director
of Battle Creek Sanitarium,
the largest hydrotherapy center
in the United States.
It was destroyed by fire in 1902.

Grandma's Lye Soap—Improved!

Saturday Night Special

Coarse oatmeal contributes plenty of character to this soap. It really scrubs skin clean and it contains starch, which is soothing to the skin. The fragrance is fine enough for any special Saturday night.

8 ounces lard
6 ounces shortening
2 ounces coconut oil

2.3 ounces lye
1/2 cup cold water

Optional ingredients:
2 tablespoons old-fashioned oatmeal (dry)
1/8 teaspoon orange soap color (prepared by the chart on page 188)

Fragrance:
3/4 teaspoon cedar wood oil
3/4 teaspoon lemon grass oil
1/2 teaspoon artificial citronella oil
1/8 teaspoon natural clove oil (leaf)

Fat temperature: 95 degrees F
Lye-water temperature: 160 degrees F
Tracing time: 1 hour
Time in molds: 24 hours
Age: 3 weeks

Skin Emollient
(for all skin types)

For softer, smoother skin,
add 1/2 cup baking soda
to the bath water.

Back-to-basics

There are no fancy frills, fillers or fragrances here—just plain soap for those who believe in life's simple pleasures.

6 ounces shortening
4 ounces beef tallow
3 ounces coconut oil
3 ounces lard

2.4 ounces lye
1 cup cold water

Fat temperature: 150 degrees F
Lye-water temperature: 165 degrees F
Tracing time: 30 minutes
Time in molds: 24 hours

Place the soap in a freezer for 3 hours, then remove it from the molds.
Age: 3 weeks

"Neat" Soap

Manufacturers boil fat and lye
for several hours to form soap.
They add salt, which causes
the soap to separate into two layers.
The top layer is called "neat" soap.
Beneath the neat soap remains
a solution which is drained off
and further processed
to obtain glycerin. Glycerin is
a valuable byproduct of soapmaking,
used to make cosmetics,
explosives and many other products.

Righteous Rose

This soap represents a bit of self-indulgence from bygone days that you can masterfully recreate for today.

8 ounces beef tallow
4 ounces coconut oil
4 ounces olive oil

2.4 ounces lye
3/4 cup cold water

Optional ingredients:
2 tablespoons tiny rose petals
1/8 teaspoon Pourette® red soap color

Fragrance:
2 teaspoons bois de rose

(Fragrance continued)
1/16 teaspoon artificial cinnamon oil
1/16 teaspoon natural clove oil (leaf)

Fat temperature: 100 degrees F
Lye-water temperature: 164 degrees F
Tracing time: 50 minutes
Time in molds: 24 hours
Place the soap in a freezer for 3 hours, then remove it from the molds.
Age: 3 weeks

Shaving Soap
Pour three or four inches
of a superfatted soap into a mug.
Wait for the soap to age and harden.
Leave the soap in the mug and
use it with a shaving brush.

Snow Tiger

Mother Nature packs oodles of cleaning power and no abrasives into borax soap. Borax is sodium tetraborate, a natural water softener mined from the earth. Capture pure, white Snow Tiger, a soap as practical as it is beautiful.

6 ounces olive oil
4 ounces lard
3 ounces shortening
2 ounces palm oil
1 ounce coconut oil

2.3 ounces lye
1 cup cold water

Optional Ingredient:
2 tablespoons powdered borax

Fragrance:
1 tablespoon Sunfeather™ Rain Perfume

Fat temperature: 120 degrees F
Lye-water temperature: 145 degrees F
Tracing time: 45 minutes
Time in molds: 3 days
Place the soap in a freezer for 12 hours, then remove it from the molds.
Age: 8 weeks

In AD 79, a volcano eruption destroyed Pompeii in southwest Italy. Archeologists uncovered a complete soapmaking factory in the ruins.

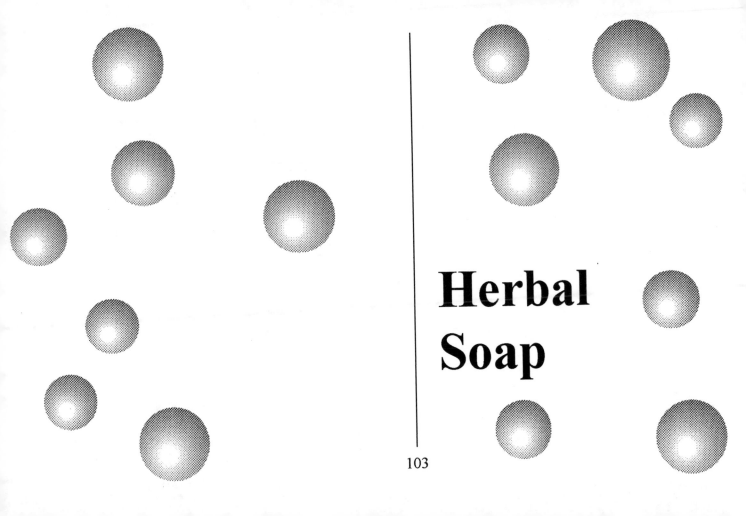

Herbal
Soap

Herbal Soap

Pure, gentle, effective soap with ingredients provided by Mother Nature herself.

105 Safflower Herbal Soap
106 Wonder Soap
107 Wild Blue Yonder
108 Green Goddess

Safflower Herbal Soap

The safflower plant is an herb of the same family as the thistle and the daisy. Oil is produced from the seeds. Safflower oil is sold with cooking oils. It's the perfect fat for truly herbal soap, especially when teamed with this fresh, herbal fragrance.

9 ounces safflower oil
4 ounces coconut oil
3 ounces palm oil
1/2 ounce beeswax

2.5 ounces lye
1 cup cold water

Fragrance:
1 teaspoon lavender oil
1 teaspoon rosemary oil
1/16 teaspoon thyme oil

Fat temperature: 160 degrees F
Lye-water temperature: 150 degrees F
Tracing time: 30 minutes
Time in molds: 24 hours
Place the soap in a freezer for 3 hours, then remove it from the molds.
Age: 3 weeks

Sebastian Kneipp, a Catholic priest of the 19th century, gained a wide reputation for his success with water cures.

Wonder Soap

Wonder Soap as in I-wonder-why-this-soap-makes-my-skin-feel-so-good. The secret is skin-healing lungwort leaf, an ugly name for *Pulmonaria officinalis* that you will learn to love. You'll also love the fifteen-minute tracing time, a wonderfully-fast time for a vegetable-based soap! Experience the wonder!

10 ounces coconut oil
3 ounces shortening
2 ounces cocoa butter
1 ounce avocado oil

2.6 ounces lye
3/4 cup cold water

Optional ingredients:
1 tablespoon lungwort leaf
1 tablespoon oatmeal baby cereal (dry)
1 teaspoon baby or mineral oil
1/16 teaspoon Pourette® green soap color

Fragrance:
1 teaspoon artificial coconut oil
1 teaspoon ylang-ylang oil
1/4 teaspoon natural lemon oil

Fat temperature: 150 degrees F
Lye-water temperature: 150 degrees F
Tracing time: 15 minutes
Time in molds: 24 hours
Age: 3 weeks

Cloves are the unopened flower
buds of a tropical tree.

Herbal Soap

Wild Blue Yonder

Get ready to soar into the Wild Blue Yonder! The fun begins with slippery elm powder, a skin-worshipping treatment that does wonders for skin. Before you slip into something more comfortable, the Wild Blue Yonder is a nice place to go.

6 ounces olive oil
3 ounces coconut oil
3 ounces shortening
2 ounces cocoa butter
1 ounce light sesame oil
1 ounce beeswax

2.3 ounces lye
1 cup cold water

Optional ingredients:
1 tablespoon bentonite clay
1 tablespoon slippery elm powder
1 teaspoon baby or mineral oil
1/8 teaspoon Pourette® blue soap color

Fragrance:
2 teaspoons ylang-ylang oil
1 teaspoon sandalwood oil
1/8 teaspoon natural clove oil (leaf)

Fat temperature: 140 degrees F
Lye-water temperature: 130 degrees F
Tracing time: 10 minutes
Time in molds: 24 hours
Place the soap in a freezer for 3 hours, then remove it from the molds.
Age: 3 weeks

Green Goddess

The ancients used lemon Balm, *Melissa officinalis,* as a symbol of gentleness and as a general cure-all. Herbalists today consider it antiseptic and calming in nature. Bentonite is an absorbent clay and wheat germ oil is a natural source of vitamin E. With so much going for it, this soap is destined for greatness!

9 ounces wheat germ oil
5 ounces coconut oil
2 ounces cocoa butter
1/2 ounce beeswax

2.5 ounces lye
1 cup cold water

Optional ingredients:
1 tablespoon bentonite clay
1 teaspoon baby or mineral oil
1 teaspoon chamomile
1 teaspoon lemon balm
1/16 teaspoon lime-green coloring
(prepared by the chart on page 188)

Fragrance:
1 1/2 teaspoons Sunfeather™
Lilac Perfume Oil
1/16 teaspoon thyme oil

Fat temperature: 160 degrees F
Lye-water temperature: 145 degrees F
Tracing time: 5 minutes
Time in molds: 24 hours
Place the soap in a freezer for 3 hours, then remove it from the molds.
Age: 8 weeks

Milk
Soap

Milk Soap

What's new from the dairy case?—soap!—milk soap to be exact.

To make milk soap, dissolve the lye in the milk, instead of the water. Don't be alarmed when the lye-milk mixture turns lumpy and orange! The lumps are casein, one of several proteins in milk. With no artificial color added, milk soap ages to become a light tan color.

111 Dynamic Duo
112 Barley Bath
113 Lagniappe
114 Luxury Bar
115 Buttercup
116 Cinnabar

Milk Soap

Dynamic Duo

Looking for a change of pace in your bath routine? Irish moss is a seaweed that provides a scrubbing action to rev circulation and invigorate skin to a polished glow. Calendula is a soothing remedy for dry, rough or chapped skin. I think you'll find that they're a Dynamic Duo for total skin care.

8 ounces coconut oil
7 ounces shortening
1 ounce cocoa butter

2.6 ounces lye
3/4 cup cold skim milk

Optional ingredients:
1 tablespoon calendula petals
1 tablespoon Irish moss (carrageen)
1/16 teaspoon salmon color
(prepared by the chart on page 188)

Fragrance:
1 1/2 teaspoons ylang-ylang oil
1/16 teaspoon thyme oil

Fat temperature: 110 degrees F
Lye-milk temperature: 155 degrees F
Tracing time: 2 minutes
Time in molds: 24 hours
Place the soap in a freezer for 3 hours, then remove it from the molds.
Age: 3 weeks

Bar soap used for bathing
is commonly called "toilet soap."

Milk Soap

Barley Bath

You've waited long enough to experience the skin-softening and heart-warming combination of milk and barley. Let yourself go with this endless source of bath time pleasure.

5 ounces coconut oil
5 ounces shortening
4 ounces beef tallow
2 ounces lard

2.5 ounces lye
1 cup cold skim milk

Optional ingredient:
1/2 cup barley baby cereal (dry)

Fragrance:
1/2 teaspoon natural clove oil (leaf)
1/2 teaspoon patchouli oil
1/2 teaspoon sassafras oil

Fat temperature: 120 degrees F
Lye-milk temperature: 150 degrees F
Tracing time: 20 minutes
This soap thickens quickly. Stir it twenty minutes before you pour it into molds.
Time in molds: 24 hours
Place the soap in a freezer for 3 hours, then remove it from the molds.
Age: 3 weeks

In one year,
the average American uses about
twenty-eight pounds
of soap and detergent.

Milk Soap

Lagniappe

Lagniappe means something extra, something unexpected and something special. That's just what this spiced milk and honey soap is—the créme de la créme of milk soap. These ingredients form a deep brown-colored soap without the use of artificial color.

9 ounces coconut oil
7 ounces beef tallow

2.6 ounces lye
3/4 cup cold skim milk

Optional ingredient:
1 teaspoon honey (add to lye and milk)

Fragrance:
1 1/2 teaspoons cinnamon oil
1/2 teaspoon natural clove oil (leaf)

Fat temperature: 90 degrees F
Lye-milk temperature: 180 degrees F
Tracing time: 45 minutes
Time in molds: 24 hours
Age: 3 weeks

Soothing Starch Bath
A starch bath is soothing to the skin and an excellent treatment for rashes. Simply add one pound of cornstarch, arrowroot or dry laundry starch to a tub of water; mix well and bathe as usual.

Milk Soap

Luxury Bar

Warm, friendly and personable are words that will come to mind as you enjoy goat milk soap. Heady, majestic and elegant are words that will come to mind as you enjoy Sunfeather's™ Musk fragrance. This refreshingly different soap is designed for luxury and pleasure.

6 ounces shortening
5 ounces cocoa butter
5 ounces coconut oil

2.5 ounces lye
1 cup goat milk
1/2 cup cold water

Fragrance:
1 1/2 teaspoons Sunfeather™
Musk Perfume Oil

Fat temperature: 110 degrees F
Lye-water-milk temperature:
165 degrees F
Tracing time: 10 minutes
Time in molds: 24 hours
Place the soap in a freezer for 3 hours, then remove it from the molds.
Age: 3 weeks

Soap needs water!
On an average day, each person in the United States uses about seventy gallons of water.

Milk Soap

Buttercup

The old-fashioned charm of milk and peanut butter combine with herbs and beeswax to blend your bath with nature.
I think you'll find this soap an easy way
to put luxury in the palm of your hand.

8 ounces shortening
4 ounces coconut oil
4 ounces lard

2.5 ounces lye
1 cup cold skim milk

Optional ingredients:
1 tablespoon calendula petals
1 tablespoon chamomile

(Optional ingredients continued)
1 teaspoon creamy peanut butter
1/8 teaspoon Pourette® yellow soap color

Fragrance:
1 1/2 teaspoons neroli perfume oil
1/2 teaspoon sassafras oil
1/8 teaspoon patchouli oil

Fat temperature: 100 degrees F
Lye-milk temperature: 150 degrees F
Tracing time: 35 minutes
Time in molds: 24 hours
Place the soap in a freezer for 3 hours,
then remove it from the molds.
Age: 3 weeks

In the Middle Ages, particularly
in Germany, the barber offered
baths as well as haircuts.

Milk Soap

Cinnabar

The dark vermilion color and spicy-sweet fragrance of soybean milk soap will cheer your very soul. I couldn't find soybean milk locally, so I ordered Walnut Acres® Powdered Soy Beverage. It contains small amounts of several additives: brown rice syrup, sunflower oil, calcium carbonate, sea salt and lecithin. Rather than interfere with the soap-making process, these additives seem to contribute to a truly luxurious soap.

6 ounces shortening
5 ounces coconut oil
3 ounces soy oil
2 ounces cocoa butter
1/4 ounce beeswax

2.4 ounces lye
3/4 cup water

Optional ingredients:
2 tablespoons soy milk powder (dry)
1/8 teaspoon Pourette® red soap color

Fragrance:
1 teaspoon cinnamon oil
1/2 teaspoon patchouli oil
1/2 teaspoon ylang-ylang oil
1/4 teaspoon natural clove oil (leaf)

Fat temperature: 150 degrees F
Lye-milk temperature: 160 degrees F
Tracing time: 6 minutes
Time in molds: 24 hours
Age: 8 weeks

Special-
purpose
Soap

Special-purpose Soap

Fun, functional and sometimes zany soap,
created with a special purpose in mind.

119 Lather Lust
120 Cedar-for-your-chest
121 E-Z Night Life
122 True Grit
123 Refreshing Rosemary
124 Anise Soap
126 Lavender-rose Luxury

Special-purpose Soap

Lather Lust

1) Lemon grass is a fresh, clean scent.
2) Sandalwood comes from East India, where it's believed to be an aphrodisiac.
3) In ancient Persia, clove oil was added to love potions. This soap has definite potential!

10 ounces canola oil
4 ounces palm oil
2 ounces coconut oil

2.3 ounces lye
1/2 cup cold water

Optional ingredient:
1 tablespoon dill weed

Fragrance:
1 teaspoon sandalwood oil
1/2 teaspoon artificial citronella oil
1/2 teaspoon lemon grass oil
1/8 teaspoon natural clove oil (leaf)

Fat temperature: 105 degrees F
Lye-water temperature: 160 degrees F
Combine the fats and lye-water; stir ten minutes. Place the soap in an oven at 200 degrees F for fifteen minutes. Stir the soap and leave it in the oven another fifteen minutes. Remove the soap from the oven and stir until it cools to 140 degrees F and traces (about twenty minutes). Add the fragrant oils and color.
Tracing time: 1 hour
Time in molds: 48 hours
Place the soap in a freezer for 12 hours, then remove it from the molds.
Age: 6 weeks

Cedar-for-your-chest

It's a surprising pleasure to experience cedar's refreshing, woodsy fragrance as a wake-me-up for morning baths. A few bars of this soap loosely wrapped in waxed paper and stored with woolens will keep moths at bay. This soap is definitely top-drawer!

10 ounces shortening
6 ounces coconut oil

2.4 ounces lye
3/4 cup cold water

Optional ingredients:
1/2 teaspoon Peruvian balsam
1/4 teaspoon orange soap color

Fragrance:
1 tablespoon cedar wood oil

Fat temperature: 120 degrees F
Lye-water temperature: 175 degrees F
Tracing time: 1 hour, 20 minutes
Time in molds: 24 hours
Place the soap in a freezer for 3 hours, then remove it from the molds.
Age: 3 weeks

Note: Stir the soap with a whisk to break-up large lumps of balsam; small lumps should remain.

> Queen Isabella of Spain
> boasted of having only two baths
> in her life: one at her birth
> and one before her wedding.

Special-purpose Soap

E-Z Night Life

Herbalists believe many essential oils are offensive to insects. This soap contains six of the best. Research proved that almost any oily substance on skin repels insects. This soap is superfatted with mineral oil.

8 ounces lard
6 ounces olive oil
2 ounces palm oil
1/4 ounce beeswax

2.3 ounces lye
1 cup cold water

Optional ingredients:
1 teaspoon mineral oil
1/8 teaspoon peach soap color

Fragrance:
1/2 teaspoon cedar wood oil
1/2 teaspoon citronella oil
1/2 teaspoon patchouli oil
1/8 teaspoon fir needle oil
1/8 teaspoon lavender oil
1/8 teaspoon pennyroyal oil

Fat temperature: 140 degrees F
Lye-water temperature: 145 degrees F
Tracing time: 40 minutes
Time in molds: 24 hours
Place the soap in a freezer for 3 hours, then remove it from the molds.
Age: 3 weeks

In 1700, there were sixty-three soapmaking companies in London.

121

Special-purpose Soap

True Grit

Combine the fresh fragrance of ground cardamom with the spiciness of ground cinnamon and pumice. What do you get?—a hand soap that gets down to the nitty-gritty when it comes to aggressive cleansing. Natural elements come together and form the perfect clean-up for whatever mess you've been into.

14 ounces coconut oil
2 ounces cocoa butter

2.8 ounces lye
1 cup cold water

Optional ingredients:
2 tablespoons 2F pumice

(Optional ingredients continued)
1 teaspoon cardamom
1 teaspoon cinnamon
1/16 teaspoon brown soap color
(prepared by the chart on page 188)

Fragrance:
1 1/2 teaspoons artificial bergamot oil

Fat temperature: 100 degrees F
Lye-water temperature: 165 degrees F
Tracing time: 1 hour, 15 minutes
Time in molds: 24 hours
Place the soap in a freezer for 3 hours, then remove it from the molds.
Age: 3 weeks

Automysophobia is
the fear of being dirty.

Refreshing Rosemary

Make thee a box
  of the wood of rosemary
and smell to it
  and it shall preserve thy youth.

This may be a somewhat exaggerated claim, but rosemary's fragrance will certainly make you feel young. Here, the strong, fresh fragrance of rosemary is tempered with a sweet touch of jasmine.

9 ounces shortening
4 ounces coconut oil
3 ounces lard

2.4 ounces lye
3/4 cup cold water

Optional ingredients:
1 teaspoon bentonite clay
1 teaspoon rosemary
1/16 teaspoon Pourette® green soap color

Fragrance:
1 1/2 teaspoons rosemary oil
1/2 teaspoon jasmine perfume oil

Fat temperature: 165 degrees F
Lye-water temperature: 165 degrees F
Tracing time: 1 hour 15 minutes
Time in molds: 24 hours
Age: 3 weeks

In your "birthday suit" means in the nude.

123

Anise Soap

Some people who fish believe anise effectively covers the human scent that scares fish away. Some bear hunters believe anise hides the human scent from bears. If you like the fragrance of licorice candy, you'll like this soap—even if you aren't into fishing or hunting.

7 ounces lard
6 ounces sunflower oil
3 ounces coconut oil
1/2 ounce beeswax

2.4 ounces lye
1/2 cup cold water

Optional ingredient:
1/2 teaspoon caraway seed

Fragrance:
1 1/2 teaspoons natural anise oil

Fat temperature: 110 degrees F
Lye-water temperature: 160 degrees F
Tracing time: 24 hours
Combine the fat and lye-water and stir the soap for ten minutes. Add the anise oil and stir the soap occasionally for two hours. Leave the soap in the stirring bowl for twenty-four hours. Add the beeswax to the soap and place it in a 200-degree oven for forty-five minutes. Stir the soap every fifteen minutes. Quickly pour the soap into molds.
Time in molds: 24 hours
Place the soap in a freezer for 3 hours, then remove it from the molds.
Age: 3 weeks

Lavender-rose Luxury

Everything about this delightfully mild soap takes a long time: a long time to trace, a long time in the molds and a long time to age. The strong, sweet fragrance and exceptionally rich lather makes it a luxury truly worth waiting for.

6 ounce sweet almond oil
5 ounces cocoa butter
5 ounces mink oil (light fraction)

2.2 ounces lye
3/4 cup water

Optional ingredients:
1/16 teaspoon grape soap color
(prepared by the chart on page 188)

Fragrance:
1 1/2 teaspoons boise de rose
1 teaspoon lavender oil
1/8 teaspoon sandalwood oil

Fat temperature: 100 degrees F
Lye-water temperature: 160 degrees F
Tracing time: 3 hours
This soap never really traces.
Do not add fillers that might sink.
Time in molds: 5 days
Place the soap in a freezer for 12 hours, then remove it from the molds.
Age: 6 weeks

> Follow a hot bath
> with cooler water to close the pores
> of the skin and to reduce
> the body temperature to normal.

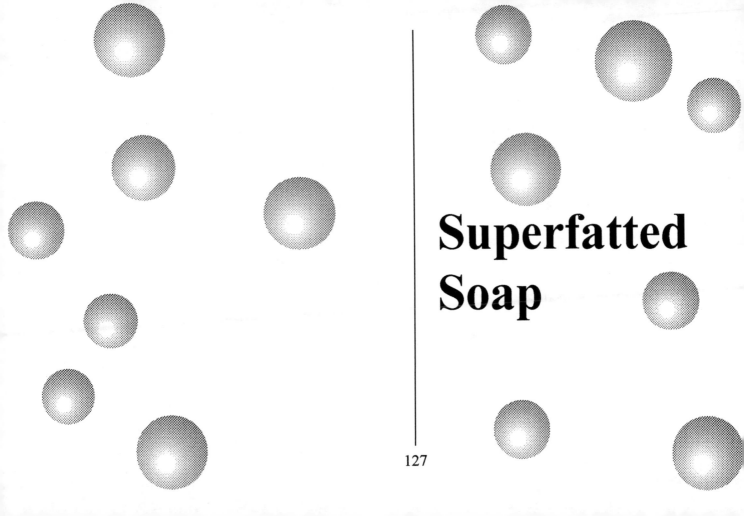

Superfatted Soap

Superfatted Soap

Superfatted soap contains excess oil that leaves a thin, protective layer on the skin. It is good for shaving and for removing make-up. It's also good for people with dry, sensitive skin.

I've seen many soap recipes that list additional lanolin, cold cream, skin lotion, cocoa butter, even castor oil to make superfatted soap. Adding extra fat to soap recipes is not a good idea. The amount of lye and fat should be perfectly balanced. Ideally, all of the lye reacts with all of the fat. Extra fat in soap can become rancid with time and make the soap smell bad, even scented soap!

The good news is that petroleum products such as baby oil, mineral oil and petroleum jelly are unaffected by lye and they don't become rancid. Read the label of brand-name soaps such as Caress® and Gentle Touch®. They contain mineral oil.

Superfatted Soap

Bois de Rose

If you enjoy gloriously sweet, floral fragrances, you heart will soar when you experience this delightful soap. Think of it as insurance against dry skin.

6 ounces coconut oil
6 ounces olive oil
5 ounces shortening

2.6 ounces lye
1 cup cold water

Optional ingredients:
1 teaspoon petroleum jelly
1/8 teaspoon Pourette® red soap color

Fragrance:
1 teaspoon bois de rose
1/2 teaspoon natural peppermint oil
1/2 teaspoon neroli perfume oil
1/2 teaspoon rosemary oil
1/8 teaspoon patchouli oil
1/8 teaspoon sandalwood oil

Fat temperature: 120 degrees F
Lye-water temperature: 160 degrees F
Tracing time: 1 hour, 30 minutes
Time in molds: 48 hours
Age: 4 weeks

Justus von Liebig, a nineteenth century German chemist, proposed that a country's soap consumption is an indication of its wealth and civilization.

The Bee's Knees

Besides being the name of a cocktail invented in London, "The Bee's Knees" was a slang expression of the 1920s meaning "super" or "smashing." Need I say more?

8 ounces shortening
6 ounces coconut oil
2 ounces walnut oil
1/2 ounce beeswax

2.5 ounces lye
1 cup cold water

Optional ingredient:
1 teaspoon baby or mineral oil

Fragrance:
1 1/2 teaspoons Sunfeather™
Lilac Perfume Oil

Fat temperature: 160 degrees F
Lye-water temperature: 150 degrees F
Tracing time: 4 minutes
Time in molds: 24 hours
Place the soap in a freezer for 3 hours, then remove it from the molds.
Age: 3 weeks

William Proctor, a soap maker, and James Gamble, a candle maker, married two women who were sisters. The men joined their trades and sold soap and candles house to house in Cincinnati during the 1800s. Their business prospered and became well-known as Proctor and Gamble®.

Superfatted Soap

Naked Sunday

The skin soothing effects of chamomile makes superfatted soap even more gentle to skin. Once you experience the soap, you will understand the name.

6 ounces coconut oil
6 ounces shortening
4 ounces rice bran oil

2.5 ounces lye
1/2 cup cold water

Optional ingredients:
1 tablespoon baby or mineral oil
1 tablespoon chamomile
1/16 teaspoon peach soap color
(prepared by the chart on page 188)

Fragrance:
1 teaspoon artificial citronella oil
1/2 teaspoon lemon grass oil
1/4 teaspoon artificial cinnamon oil
1/8 teaspoon sandalwood oil

Fat temperature: 115 degrees F
Lye-water temperature: 160 degrees F
Tracing time: 30 minutes

Combine the fats and lye-water; stir ten minutes. Place the soap in an oven at 200 degrees F for fifteen minutes. Remove the soap from the oven and stir until it cools to 160 degrees F and traces (about five minutes). Stir in the fragrant oils and optional ingredients. Pour the soap into molds.

Time in molds: 24 hours
Age: 3 weeks

Superfatted Soap

Morning Dove

Greet the morning with the skin-pampering oils of Morning Dove. It's a welcomed relief for dry skin that makes you feel good all over.

Set oven at 200 degrees F

7 ounces peanut oil
5 ounces coconut oil
4 ounces shortening

2.4 ounces lye
3/4 cup cold water

Optional ingredient:
1 teaspoon mineral oil

Fragrance:
1 teaspoon artificial bergamot oil
1 teaspoon lemon grass oil

Fat temperature: 115 degrees F
Lye-water temperature: 160 degrees F
Tracing time: 1 hour, 20 minutes

Preheat an oven to 200 degrees F. Add the lye-water to the fat and put it in the oven for one hour; stir every fifteen minutes. Remove the soap from the oven. This soap tries to separate, so instead of stirring it with a rubber spatula, stir it with a whisk for ten minutes or until the soap cools to 150 degrees F and traces. Add the optional ingredients and mold.

Time in molds: 24 hours
Age: 6 weeks

Decongestant Soap

This is an usual recipe for an unusual soap. It's a gentle decongestant with loads of lather.

6 ounces coconut oil
6 ounces shortening
2 ounces cocoa butter
2 ounces light sesame oil

2.5 ounces lye
1/2 cup cold water

Optional ingredients:
2 tablespoons Mentholatum®
      or Vicks VapoRub®
1/16 teaspoon Pourette® blue color

Fat temperature: 140 degrees F
Lye-water temperature: 125 degrees F
Tracing time: 45 minutes
Time in molds: 3 days
Place the soap in a freezer for 3 hours, then remove it from the molds.
Age: 3 weeks

In 1806, William Colgate bought a kettle that could hold 45,000 pounds of soap. His business, Colgate and Company, became the largest soap manufacturer in the United States.

Pure Vanilla Pleasure

Sit back and enjoy the warm vanilla fragrance of this honest-to-goodness soap—simple, yet so satisfying.

8 ounces coconut oil
8 ounces shortening
1/2 ounce beeswax

2.6 ounces lye
1 cup cold water

Optional ingredient:
1 teaspoon baby or mineral oil

Fragrance:
2 teaspoons vanillin powder, USP

(Fragrance continued)
1 teaspoon Peruvian balsam

Fat temperature: 150 degrees F
Lye-water temperature: 150 degrees F
Tracing time: 3 minutes
Time in molds: 24 hours
Place the soap in a freezer for 3 hours, then remove it from the molds.
Age: 3 weeks

Note: Stir the soap with a whisk to break up large lumps of balsam.

Today, lye is made by a process known as *electrolysis*, which consists of passing an electric current through a salt solution to cause a chemical reaction.

Superfatted Soap

Gentle Jasmine

This soap is excellent for dry skin. It doesn't lather as well as most of the soap made from the recipes in this book, but the gentleness and sweet fragrance makes it definitely worthwhile.

6 ounces castor oil
5 ounces coconut oil
5 ounces palm oil

2.5 ounces lye
1/2 cup cold water

Optional ingredients:
1 teaspoon baby or mineral oil
1/4 cup baby oatmeal cereal (dry)

Fragrance:
2 teaspoons jasmine perfume oil
1/4 teaspoon artificial citronella oil
1/4 teaspoon sandalwood oil

Fat temperature: 95 degrees F
Lye-water temperature: 180 degrees F
Tracing time: 1 hour, 30 minutes

Mix the fats and lye-water and stir occasionally for fifteen minutes. Place the soap in a preheated 200-degree oven for forty-five minutes; stir every fifteen minutes. Remove the soap from the oven and stir it occasionally until it traces (about thirty minutes). Add the optional ingredients and mold.

Time in molds: 2 days
Place the soap in a freezer for 3 hours, then remove it from the molds.
Age: 3 weeks

"Exactly how many sunflower seeds did you put in this soap, dear?"

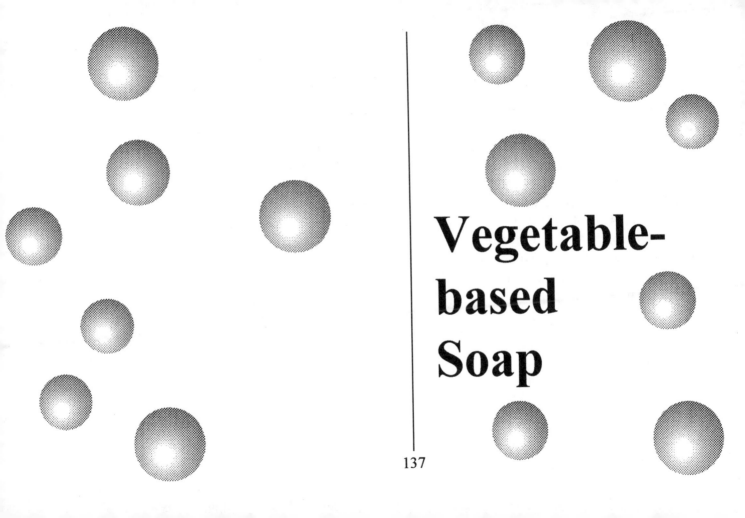

Vegetable-based Soap

Vegetable-based Soap

Veggie lovers take note!
Here is a solution for hard-to-find soaps designed to complement a healthy diet and lifestyle. No artificial color, animal fat or petroleum products are necessary in this soap! There are many vegetable-based recipes throughout this book, but this chapter is devoted entirely to you. By the way, if you hear a rumor that soap from vegetable oil is soft and doesn't last long—don't you believe it! Here are the recipes that prove my point.

Vegetable-based Soap

Sunflower Soap

Sunflower Soap is as warm and cheerful as its namesake—a little bit of sunshine in every bar. The sweet-patchouli fragrance remains as strong as on the day the soap was made.

12 ounces sunflower oil
4 ounces shortening

2.2 ounces lye
1/2 cup cold water

Optional ingredients:
1 tablespoon sunflower seeds (pressed and ground to a paste-like consistency)
1/8 teaspoon Pourette® yellow soap color

Fragrance:
1 teaspoon cedar wood oil
1 teaspoon patchouli oil
1/4 teaspoon jasmine perfume oil
1/4 teaspoon neroli perfume oil

Fat temperature: 100 degrees F
Lye-water temperature: 160 degrees F
Tracing time: 1 hour, 45 minutes
Add the lye-water to the fats and stir about five minutes. Place the soap in an preheated 200-degree oven at for one hour and fifteen minutes; stir it every fifteen minutes. Remove the soap from the oven and stir it fairly often until it cools and traces (about thirty minutes). Stir in the optional ingredients and pour the soap into molds.
Time in molds: 6 days
Place the soap in a freezer overnight, then remove it from the molds.
Age: 8 weeks

Vegetable-based Soap

Blue Midnight

This elegant soap is almost black, yet it produces white lather. The mystery is further enhanced with a mystic fragrance.

5 ounces coconut oil
5 ounces shortening
5 ounces sweet almond oil
1 ounce cocoa butter
1/2 ounce beeswax

2.5 ounces lye
3/4 cup cold water

Optional ingredient:
1/2 teaspoon Pourette® blue soap color

Fragrance:
1 teaspoon natural clove oil (leaf)
1 teaspoon rosemary oil

Fat temperature: 140 degrees F
Lye-water temperature: 135 degrees F
Tracing time: 5 minutes
Time in molds: 24 hours
Place the soap in a freezer for 3 hours, then remove it from the molds.
Age: 4 weeks

In the 1600s, people who spent
as long as 124 hours
in baths believed it was a treatment
to ensure good health.

Vegetable-based Soap

Rosemary Maize

Maize is Indian corn. Maize Soap not only contains corn oil, but blue corn meal as well. The light "rose-merry" fragrance will keep you cheerful and refreshed.

8 ounces corn oil
6 ounces coconut oil
2 ounces palm oil

2.5 ounces lye
1/2 cup cold water

Optional ingredients:
1 tablespoon blue cornmeal
1 teaspoon baby or mineral oil
1/8 teaspoon grape soap color
(prepared by the chart on page 188)

Fragrance:
1 1/2 teaspoons rosemary oil
1/2 teaspoon lemon grass oil
1/8 teaspoon sandalwood oil

Fat temperature: 115 degrees F
Lye-water temperature: 160 degrees F
Tracing time: 45 minutes

Combine the fat and lye-water; stir for ten minutes. Place the soap in a preheated 200-degree oven for thirty minutes; stir at fifteen minutes. Remove the soap from the oven and add optional ingredients. Stir it for about five minutes or until it cools to 180 degrees F and traces.

Time in molds: 24 hours
Place the soap in a freezer for 3 hours, then remove it from the molds.
Age: 4 weeks

141

Vegetable-based Soap

Sweet Hesitation

Sweet Hesitation is so soothing you'll hesitate to leave the bath! It contains chamomile, which herbalists consider a skin-moisturizing toner. I added Celestial Seasonings® chamomile tea straight from the bag—no grinding necessary. Whether taken as tea, or put in the bath, chamomile is one of the most relaxing herbs.

10 ounces corn oil
6 ounces palm oil

2.3 ounces lye
1/2 cup cold water

Optional ingredient:
1 tablespoon chamomile

Fragrance:
1 teaspoon neroli perfume oil
1/2 teaspoon ylang-ylang oil
1/4 teaspoon artificial bergamot oil
1/4 teaspoon artificial cinnamon oil

Fat temperature: 125 degrees F
Lye-water temperature: 160 degrees F
Tracing time: 1 hour
Combine the fats and lye-water; stir ten minutes. Place the soap in a preheated 200-degree oven for fifteen minutes. Stir the soap and leave it in the oven another fifteen minutes. Remove the soap from the oven and stir until it cools to 140 degrees F and traces (about fifteen minutes).
Stir in the fragrant oils and pour the soap into molds.
Time in molds: 24 hours
Place the soap in a freezer for 3 hours, then remove it from the molds.
Age: 6 weeks

Vegetable-based Soap

Earthnut Soap

Earthnut is an old-fashioned name for peanut. As you probably guessed, this down-to-earth soap contains peanut oil. This soap is naturally white. The brown color is optional.

Set the oven at 200 degrees F.

24 8 ounces peanut oil
12 4 ounces coconut oil
12 4 ounces shortening

7.2 2.4 ounces lye
12.6 1/2 cup cold water

Optional ingredient:
1/16 teaspoon brown soap color

Fragrance:
1 teaspoon sassafras oil
1/2 teaspoon lemon grass oil
1/2 teaspoon neroli perfume oil
1/2 teaspoon rosemary oil

Fat temperature: 125 degrees F
Lye-water temperature: 160 degrees F
Combine the fats and lye-water. Stir for about ten minutes. Place the soap in a preheated 200-degree oven for fifteen minutes. Stir the soap and leave it in the oven another fifteen minutes. Remove the soap from the oven and stir until it cools to 140 degrees F and traces (about fifteen minutes). Stir in the fragrant oils and pour the soap into molds.
Tracing time: 1 hour
Time in molds: 24 hours
Place the soap in a freezer for 3 hours, then remove it from the molds.
Age: 4 weeks

Vegetable-based Soap

Rub-a-dub-dub

No exotic fragrance, no fancy fillers—
what does this soap have going for it?—
a short tracing time and lots and lots of
elegant, velvety lather! With this soap in
your bath, you'll never get rubbed the
wrong way.

6 ounces shortening
5 ounces olive oil
4 ounces coconut oil
1 ounce cocoa butter
1/2 ounce beeswax

2.4 ounces lye
3/4 cup cold water

Optional ingredient:
1/4 teaspoon salmon soap color

Fat temperature: 150 degrees F
Lye-water temperature: 150 degrees F
Tracing time: 20 minutes
Time in molds: 48 hours
Place the soap in a freezer 12 hours, then
remove it from the molds.
Age: 4 weeks

"Soap" in many languages	
English	Soap
Dutch	Sepo
French	Savon
German	Seife
Hungarian	Szappan
Italian	Sapone
Latin	Sapo
Spanish	Jabón
Turkish	Sabun

Vegetable-based Soap

Pure Soap

Pure soap is free of coloring and fragrance. It's made from 100% coconut oil, which makes a very hard soap that cuts grease and produces the best lather of any handmade soap. Once you try Pure Soap, you'll wonder how you ever managed without it.

16 ounces coconut oil

2.9 ounces lye
1/2 cup cold water

Fat temperature: 90 degrees F
Lye-water temperature: 180 degrees F
Tracing time: 1 hour, 50 minutes

Combine the lye-water and the fat; stir occasionally for one hour and forty minutes. Add 1/4 cup hot tap water and stir for ten minutes.
Add another 1/4 cup hot tap water and stir until the soap is thick and smooth (a few minutes).
Time in molds: 24 hours
Place the soap in a freezer for 3 hours, then remove it from the molds.
Age: 3 weeks

You can make many cleaning products from Pure Soap. See page 162 for:
spray cleanser
laundry powder
soft-scrub cleanser
toilet bowl cleanser
jewelry cleaner
and much more!

145

Vegetable-based Soap

Oh, yes!— Sweet Almond

When a friend asked me to develop
a recipe to make soap from sweet almond
oil, I was skeptical:

- Could I create a recipe that works?
- Would sweet almond oil alone result
  in a hard bar of soap?
- Would the soap produce rich lather?

The answers are: yes!—yes!—oh, yes!
Here's the recipe for a truly world class
soap, very similar to castile, but ivory
white in color.

16 ounces sweet almond oil

2.2 ounces lye

3/4 cup cold water

Fragrance:
1 1/2 teaspoons jasmine perfume oil
1/4 teaspoon citronella oil

Fat temperature: 115 degrees F
Lye-water temperature: 160 degrees F
Tracing time: 2 days
Time in molds: 5 days
Age: 6 weeks

Add the lye-water to the fat. Put the soap
in a preheated 200-degree oven for one
hour; stir it every fifteen minutes. Remove
the soap from the oven and leave it in the
stirring bowl for two days. Stir the soap
as much as you like, but at least twice
daily. Stir in the fragrant oil, pour the
soap into molds and leave it five days.
Place the soap in a freezer for twelve
hours, then remove it from the molds; age
six weeks.

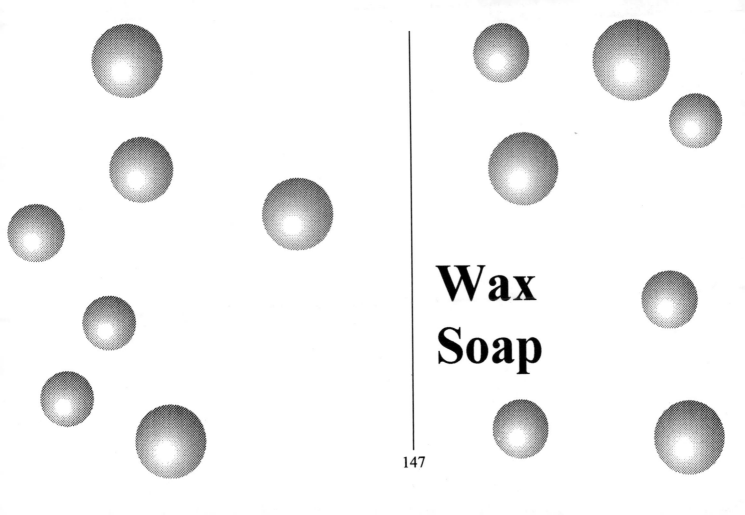

**Wax
Soap**

Wax Soap

Many waxes can be saponified (turned to soap) just like the more familiar fats. Until now, only a fortunate few have reveled in the richness of wax soaps. Waxes such as bayberry, beeswax and carnauba are expensive and seldom added to commercial soap. It's a shame too, because wax soap is hard and very smooth-textured. Wax soap doesn't dissolve as quickly as most handmade soap; therefore, it lasts longer. These recipes will put luxury at your fingertips.

The Inspired Soap Creator

Wax Soap

Frisky Frolic

Capture the splendor of an exotic vacation without leaving home. Cocoa butter is the ticket for smoother skin, while the mysteriously sweet fragrance takes you anywhere you want to go.

9 ounces olive oil
7 ounces cocoa butter
1/2 ounce bayberry or myrtle wax

2.2 ounces lye
3/4 cup cold water

Fragrance:
1 teaspoon bois de rose
1/2 teaspoon lavender oil
1/8 teaspoon natural clove oil (leaf)

(Fragrance continued)
1/8 teaspoon sandalwood oil

Fat temperature: 100 degrees F
Lye-water temperature: 140 degrees F
Tracing time: 10 minutes
Time in molds: 24 hours
Place the soap in a freezer for 3 hours, then remove it from the molds.
Age: 4 weeks

Nicholas Leblanc (1742–1806), a French physician and industrial chemist, melted together sodium sulfate, limestone and coal to produce lye economically. In 1794, the French revolutionary government seized Leblanc's patent and his factory. Although many persons made fortunes by using his process, Leblanc lived in poverty.

Bayberry Castile

Bayberry is a fragrant wax from a North American shrub, *Myrica pensylvanica*. Bayberry wax plus olive oil equals a naturally-colored soap. The light olive-green color is a good base for herbal soap that doesn't require artificial color.

10 ounces olive oil
4 ounces palm oil
2 ounces coconut oil
2 ounces bayberry or myrtle wax

2.5 ounces lye
1 cup cold water

Fragrance:
1 teaspoon neroli perfume oil

(Fragrance continued)
1/4 teaspoon lemon grass oil
1/8 teaspoon natural clove oil (leaf)
1/8 teaspoon sandalwood oil

Fat temperature: 165 degrees F
Lye-water temperature: 145 degrees F
Tracing time: 4 minutes
Time in molds: 24 hours
Place the soap in a freezer for 3 hours, then remove it from the molds.
Age: 8 weeks

In 1852, a heavy tax
on English soap was lifted by
Chancellor of the Exchequer Gladstone.
He said, "…a clean nation
is a happy nation."

Wax Soap

Spermaceti Soap

Discover the richness of Spermaceti Soap. Spermaceti is a white, waxy material once used in ointments and cosmetics. Artificial spermaceti is similarly wax-like, less-expensive and the wax used to test this recipe. This smooth-textured, hard soap is long-lasting as is the unusual and delightful spearmint-patchouli fragrance.

6 ounces canola oil
6 ounces coconut oil
2 ounces palm oil
2 ounces spermaceti
1 ounce beef tallow

2.4 ounces lye
3/4 cup cold water

Optional ingredient:
1/16 teaspoon Pourette® green soap color

Fragrance:
1 teaspoon natural spearmint oil
1 teaspoon patchouli oil

Fat temperature: 135 degrees F
Lye-water temperature: 160 degrees F
Tracing time: 1 hour, 30 minutes
Time in molds: 24 hours
Place the soap in a freezer for 3 hours, then remove it from the molds.
Age: 3 weeks

In 1776, soap- and candle-making were kindred trades as both were made with tallow.

Wax Soap

Peachy Keen

A bit of Pourette® red soap color (about the size of this capital "O") combines with the natural yellow of beeswax to equal a beautiful peach-colored soap. Dissolve the coloring in the flavoring oil. Use only peach flavoring *oil* for this recipe and not the more familiar peach flavoring *extract*, which contains too much alcohol.

6 ounces olive oil
5 ounces shortening
3 ounces coconut oil
2 ounces palm oil
1 ounce beeswax

2.4 ounces lye
1 cup cold water

Fragrance:
2 teaspoons Lorann™
        Peach Flavoring Oil

Fat temperature: 160 degrees F
Lye-water temperature: 140 degrees F
Tracing time: 4 minutes
Time in molds: 24 hours
Place the soap in a freezer for 3 hours, then remove it from the molds.
Age: 6 weeks

Bath temperatures in degrees Fahrenheit	
Very cold (shocking)	32 to 55
Cold (limit to 5 minutes)	55 to 65
Cool (limit to 10 minutes)	65 to 80
Tepid	80 to 92
Warm (relaxing 30 to 60 minutes)	92 to 98
Hot (can cause itching)	98 to 104
Very hot (foot baths)	104 to 110
Dangerous	115 and up

Pollen Pleasure

You're in for a pleasant surprise! Protein-rich pollen provides gentle scrubbing grains and a natural honey color to this unusual soap.

About thirty minutes before you mix this soap, combine the fragrant oils and pollen so the pollen has time to soften. Some granules dissolve, while a few remain whole to add color and interesting texture to your Pollen Pleasure—definitely not just another soap!

9 ounces shortening
4 ounces coconut oil
3 ounces lard
1/4 ounce beeswax

2.4 ounces lye
3/4 cup cold water

Optional ingredients:
1 tablespoon natural bee pollen
1 teaspoon honey (added to the lye-water)

Fragrance:
1 teaspoon artificial bergamot oil
1/2 teaspoon sandalwood oil

Fat temperature: 155 degrees F
Lye-water temperature: 155 degrees F
Tracing time: 12 minutes
Time in molds: 24 hours
Place the soap in a freezer for 3 hours, then remove it from the molds.
Age: 3 weeks

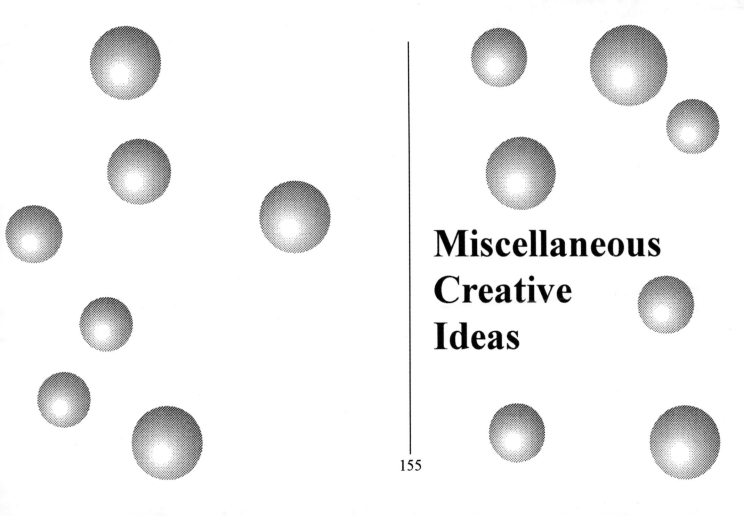

Miscellaneous Creative Ideas

Miscellaneous Creative Ideas

Soapmaking is fun and exciting, but even more creativity beacons!

Soap Shampoo

Throughout history, the best shampoos were made from pure castile soap. Common-sense hair care never goes out of style. The recipes on pages 63, 64 and 65 make good shampoo bars. For beautiful hair, simply shampoo your hair as normal. Follow the shampoo with one of the two rinses below to remove soap residue.

For light hair
1 tablespoon lemon juice
1 cup warm water

For dark hair
1 tablespoon vinegar
1 cup warm water

Optional herbal rinses
After the lemon or vinegar rinse, rinse the hair again with clear water. If you enjoy using herbs, use one of the following infusions instead of water.

For light hair
2 tablespoons chamomile
4 cups water
optional: 2 drops laundry bluing (for gray or white hair)

For dark hair
2 tablespoons rosemary or sage
4 cups water

Prepare infusions like herbal teas. Pour boiling water over the herb, cover it and let it steep for five minutes. Strain the herb from the water; wait for the water to cool and use the water as a rinse.

Layered Soap

Pouring layers of colored soap is a quick
and easy way to make unusual soap.

Here are the steps to make layered soap.

Step 1. Make some soap and fill the molds
only one-fourth to one-third full.

Step 2. After twenty-four hours, or when
the soap is firm, prepare a different color
soap and pour another layer. Add more
layers to fill the mold. It is best to complete all the layers within five days so they
will stick together.

Step 3. Age layered soap for the longest
time specified in the various recipes used
to make it.

Monograms and Designs

Here's how to make the monogrammed soap pictured on page 83.

Step 1. Begin with a dark-colored soap that has been out of the mold a few days. It should be firm enough to slice easily, but not pasty. Slice off a piece about one-half inch thick.

Step 2. Draw or trace a design onto the soap. Cut out the design with a thin-bladed knife.

Step 3. Lay the design in the bottom of a soap mold and press it down lightly. The bottom of the mold becomes the top of the soap. Be sure the design faces the right direction.

Step 4. Prepare a light-colored soap. (I used the recipe on page 83.) Pour the soap over the design and fill the mold. Continue as the soap recipe directs to remove the soap and age it.

Marbled Soap

Some colors are more suitable for marbled soap than others. You can't go wrong with one color plus white. See Appendix G, page 191, for the results of mixing other colors.

Here's how to make marbled soap.

Step 1. Choose a recipe with a tracing time between twenty minutes and one hour. Recipes with shorter tracing times don't allow enough time to "play" with the soap before it hardens.

Step 2. Make the soap as the recipe directs and divide it into two or three parts. Color each part as desired.

Step 3. Use a stainless steel spoon to alternately add each color to the mold. If the colors aren't mixed enough, you can swirl the soap while it is in the mold.

Soap Leaves

Introducing go-anywhere soap!
Soap leaves fit nicely into small envelopes
to carry with you. You'll always have
your favorite soap!

To make soap leaves, begin with soap that
has been out of the mold a few days. It
should be firm enough to slice easily, but
not pasty.

Cut the soap into very thin slices (about
1/8-inch thick) and lay it aside. Age soap
leaves the time specified in the recipe used
to make them.

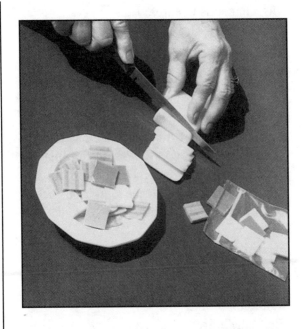

Soap leaves are very thin and really don't
contain much soap, but you'll be surprised
how much lather they produce! Discard
the wet soap after using it.

Pure Soap Products

Pure Soap (page 145) makes the best cleaning products. Here are some ideas for cleaning, but I'll bet once you start using Pure Soap, you'll develop formulas of your own. Just remember: don't combine ammonia and chlorine laundry bleach and don't combine soap and detergent.

Mixture for mopping floors

1/2 cup Pure Soap
1 teaspoon lemon grass or fir needle oil
1 gallon hot water.
Blend the ingredients in a bucket. Saturate a mop or sponge with the mixture to clean floors and walls.

Spray cleanser

1 tablespoon Pure Soap
2 tablespoons household ammonia
1 cup hot water
Combine ingredients in a spray bottle and leave it until the soap dissolves. Spray the cleanser onto dirty surfaces and wipe the area clean.

Laundry powder

1 cup grated Pure Soap
1/2 cup borax
Combine the ingredients and use 1 1/2 cups per wash load. Add 1/4 cup vinegar to the fabric softener dispenser to remove soap residue and leave clothes soft and fluffy. The smell of vinegar disappears as the clothes dry.

To clean and sanitize garbage containers

3 tablespoons chlorine laundry bleach
1/4 cup grated Pure Soap
4 cups hot water
Mix the ingredients. Clean the container with the mixture and keep the surface wet for ten minutes; rinse.

To clean walls and floors

1 cup household ammonia
1/4 cup grated Pure Soap
1/2 cup borax
2 gallons warm water
Mix the ingredients and clean walls and floors. It is not necessary to rinse.

For delicate hand washables

1/4 cup borax
1/4 cup grated Pure Soap
Add the ingredients to a basin of warm water. Soak the washables for ten minutes; rinse and blot dry with a towel.

Dish soap

Grate Pure Soap and use it for washing dishes. Instead of grating soap, you can put a bar of soap in a bowl and run hot water over it. When the bowl fills, empty it and fill it again. This makes enough liquid soap for one sink of dishes and makes grating the soap unnecessary.

Soft-scrub cleanser

1/2 cup borax
1/2 cup grated Pure Soap
Mix the ingredients. Sprinkle the mixture onto a wet surface and rub to clean it; rinse with clear water.

To clean and deodorize toilet bowls

1/4 cup borax
2 tablespoons grated Pure Soap
1/4 cup chlorine laundry bleach
Add the ingredients to one toilet bowl and swish to mix. Let it stand at least thirty minutes; overnight is best.

Foot soak for calluses

1/4 cup Pure Soap
1 tablespoon chlorine laundry bleach
1 gallon warm water
Combine the ingredients and soak your feet as long as desired.

Jewelry cleaner

1 tablespoon Pure Soap
1/4 cup household ammonia
1/4 cup water
Combine the ingredients and let the mixture stand until the soap dissolves. Soak jewelry in the cleaner for twenty minutes; rinse it and wipe it dry.

Soap for delicate washables

1/2 cup grated Pure Soap
1 tablespoon household ammonia
2 quarts hot water
Combine the ingredients in hot water to dissolve the soap. Add delicate washables when the water is warm.

Soft-scrubbing cleanser

2 tablespoons baking soda
1 tablespoon Pure Soap
1 tablespoon water or
        chlorine laundry bleach (optional
        to kill mildew)
Make a paste of the ingredients and use it to clean bathtubs, tiles, sinks and counters; rinse with clear water. This cleanser will not scratch fiberglass.

Sanitizer
(for non-porous food contact surfaces (such as sinks and counter tops)

1 tablespoon grated Pure Soap
2 tablespoons chlorine laundry bleach
1 gallon warm water
Mix the ingredients. Apply the sanitizer to a clean surface. Maintain wet surface contact for at least two minutes. I find that it's convenient to apply this mixture from a spray bottle.

Washballs

Step 1. Choose any recipe and prepare the soap. When it traces, leave it in the stirring bowl. It will gradually harden to a clay-like consistency. The trick is to catch the soap when it is the right consistency.

Step 2. Wear rubber gloves and form the soap into balls. Two or three inches is a good size; larger balls are hard to hold in your hand. Wet the gloves to keep soap from sticking to them. Don't worry if the balls look "spiky," You can smooth them later when they harden. You can also wash them smooth after they age.

Step 3. Age washballs the time specified in the recipe. See the following page for suggested additives.

Washballs are hand-formed balls of soap that were popular with eighteenth-century nobility.

(Washballs continued)

The clay-like consistency of soap necessary to make washballs provides a perfect opportunity to include additives. I don't want to hinder your creativity. Instead of recipes, here is a list of possible additives. Just be sure that everything you add is finely ground. Have fun creating your own twenty-first century recipes.

almond meal
aloe vera powder
bentonite clay
buttermilk, dry powder
calamus root, finely ground
chamomile, finely ground
clay
coloring powder
cornmeal, finely ground

dry baby cereal, any variety
dry laundry starch
elderflowers, finely ground
essential oils
fuller's earth
herbs, powdered
instant potato flakes
kaolin
lavender flowers, powdered
oatmeal, finely ground
orange flower water
orris root, powdered
rose water
rosin (pine resin)
sandalwood powder
starch
talc
ulmus (slippery elm) powder
vanillin powder
vitamin E oil
wheat germ oil

Let's Talk...

Troubleshooting
Begin your own business
Frequently asked questions

"Everything I know, I learned from experience—
never put soap in a microwave oven!"

Troubleshooting—What can go wrong?

I'd like to believe that this appendix is unnecessary because your soap will be perfect. Since the real world doesn't always operate smoothly, let's look at some things that can go wrong.

The major cause of problems

The major cause of problems or faults in the finished soap is inaccurate ingredients, weights or measures. It's easy to measure 1/2 cup water when the recipe states 3/4 cup. You can lose track of what ingredients are already in the stirring bowl and what is not yet added. You can forget to add an ingredient. I'm not saying you're inept—I often forget to add the fragrant oil. It's just that mistakes happen, especially if you're in a hurry or distracted. Of course, at the time, you don't realize you're making a mistake (else you would correct it), and when the soap doesn't turn out quite right, you wonder what went wrong.

The mixture curdles.

Soap progresses from thin and watery to thick and opaque, but the mixture should always be smooth. Curdles are thick lumps of soap in a watery mixture. For a better idea of curdles, add one tablespoon vinegar or lemon juice to one cup of milk and let it stand for five minutes. That's curdled milk and curdled soap doesn't look much different. A soap mixture can curdle when the temperature is too high and when the mixture contains too little water. Rapidly stir curdled soap with a whisk and when the mixture is smooth, pour it into molds. The soap may turn out quite good after all.

The soap doesn't release from the mold.
Properly made soap should release easily from molds that are clean (dry and oil-free). If the soap doesn't release, place it in a freezer for a few hours and try again to remove it. If the soap still doesn't release, leave it in a freezer twenty-four hours and try again.

The soap doesn't harden.
Did you wait the aging time specified in the recipe? Soap hardens as it ages; the older the soap, the harder the soap. Too much water in soap can lengthen the time it takes to harden. If there isn't enough lye in the mixture, or if the lye-water and fat temperatures are too low, the soap may never harden.

The pH tests above 10 or below 8.
The only mistake that can cause soap to be too harsh (above pH 10) or too fatty (below pH 8) is inaccurately weighing and measuring the ingredients. Soap above pH 10 is harsh to skin and should not be used for bathing. As long as the pH is not above 12, you can grate the soap and use it for cleaning purposes. (Wear rubber gloves when you use it.) Soap with a pH of 7 or less will not react with water and produce lather. It contains excess fat which (with time) can become rancid.

Clear oil comes to the surface of the soap while it's in the mold.
In some recipes, the fragrant oil tries to separate while the soap is in the molds. This is normal, so don't worry about it. Leave the soap undisturbed. Often the soap reabsorbs the oil. The thinner the soap when poured into molds, the more possibility this problem will occur. Some essential oils (anise, lemon and pine) can cause this problem.

The soap doesn't trace.
Inaccurate temperatures, measures and weights can cause this problem. There's not much hope for success if the ratio of ingredients is off. If the ingredients are correct, then inaccurate temperatures are not a serious problem. Leave the soap in the mixing bowl until it traces, no matter how long it takes. A week is not too long to wait. The soap could turn out good after all.

The corners of the bar are missing. There are holes in the outer edge.
This is caused by waiting too long to pour the soap into molds. The mixture is too thick and it doesn't flow properly to fill the mold. The soap is probably still good; it's just not very attractive. You can use the soap as it is, or cut it to make Confetti Soap (page 80).

The texture of the bar is uneven.

Properly made soap should be the same throughout: no layers evident and no small bubbles or pockets of water. These indicate a severe problem of inaccurate temperatures, weights and measures. Do not use the soap.

The soap cracks.

None of the soap I made from these recipes cracked. When I tested other recipes, I learned that a lot of shortening or palm oil in a recipe can cause soap to crack. Too little water in a mixture can also cause this problem.

The soap smells "fatty."

Did you wait the aging time specified in the recipe before you judged the scent?
Did you add the fragrant oil? If the answer to these two questions is, "Yes," then the problem is too much fat or not enough lye. Soap never turns rancid; excess fat does.

BYOB (Begin your own business)

If you'd like to sell soap, here are a few words of advice to get you started on the right track.

Choose a business image.
Your business image is the philosophy or theme you set for your business. Will it be earthy and natural, rich and luxurious, down-home and country, up-beat and modern, new age or herbal? The choices are endless, but whatever your image, reflect it in everything you do: selecting recipes, naming the soap, producing a label, advertising, selecting stationery, etc. As you choose an image, keep in mind that certain images attract certain customers.

Choose a recipe that will appeal to many customers.
Many people want to avoid animal products, petroleum products, artificial color and synthetic fragrances. The best-selling soap is likely to be a vegetable-based soap, lightly scented with a fragrance that appeals to men and women. In choosing a recipe consider the cost of ingredients, their availability and whether or not you can buy them wholesale. The cost to produce some of the recipes in this book is quite high. If your business image is based on luxury appeal to wealthy customers, perhaps you can successfully market expensive soap. If your image is down-home and country, your customers may be shocked by high prices.

Start small!
Make a one-pound test batch of the recipe chosen. Note any problems you may run into if you tripled the recipe. For instance, a recipe for a one-pound batch of soap that gets very thick within the first two minutes, may not allow enough time to get a three-pound batch of soap poured into molds.

Evaluate the shelf-life and quality of the soap.
Fragrances can disappear and soap can begin to smell "fatty." For a business, soap must have a long shelf life. Soap that retains its shape and fragrance for three months is likely to remain top quality for years. This three-month evaluation should also include a pH test. Never sell soap that tests higher than 10. The core of soap is sometimes a different color or texture than the rest of the bar. Cut or grate one bar of soap to be sure the color and texture is even throughout.

Design a unique package.
The fun part of marketing your own soap is designing a unique package.
The label should list the ingredients, in order of content from most to least.
Do not make medicinal claims about the soap or you'll find yourself answering to regulators that require scientific proof of such claims. If you wrap soap, be sure the wrapper is color-fast (colored tissue paper is not). Include your name, address and telephone number on the wrapper so your customers can locate you when they want to buy more soap.

Price your product.

Do not base the price of your luxurious handmade soap on the price of commercially produced bath bars! Your handmade soap is a unique product; rare and valuable. Price it accordingly. In my opinion, and based on the current economy in the United States, hand-made soap shouldn't be sold for less than $3.00 per 3.5-ounce bar, no matter what it cost to produce. Your price may be higher, depending on the type of soap. The selling price should include all costs plus a profit margin.

Do your homework (recommended reading).

My business advice covers only soap, the product aspect. There are many other things to consider. The following books can help you begin and successfully operate a home-based business:

- *The Basic Guide to Selling Arts and Crafts* by James Dillehay
- *Soapmaking and the Creative Art of Business* by Sandy Main (video also available)
- *Small Time Operator*: *How to start your own small business, keep your books and stay out of trouble* by Bernard Kamoroff
- *Homemade Money*: *How to select, start, manage, market and multiply the profits of a business at home* by Barbara Brabec
- *The Complete Guide to Owning a Home-based Business* from the Editors of Entrepreneur Magazine

Frequently asked questions

How can I make transparent soap?
I'd be happy to tell you—if I knew! Pourette® sells blocks of glycerin soap. All you do is melt it, pour it into the mold of your choice and wait for it to cool. It's not very creative, but it's one sure way to get transparent soap.

Is it true that I shouldn't mix soap and detergent?
It's true. The cleansing action of soap works in an opposite way of the cleansing action of detergent. Since they oppose one another, don't mix them or otherwise use them at the same time.

I've read that coconut oil causes dry skin. Why do you use so much of it?
Any oil can protect skin by forming a moisture barrier that keeps skin from drying out, even coconut oil. I believe coconut oil developed a reputation for being harsh because it takes more lye to convert it to soap than any other oil used for soapmaking. For instance:
- 2.9 ounces lye is required to convert 1 pound of coconut oil to soap
- 2.2 ounces lye is required to convert 1 pound of olive oil to soap

The pH of the two types of soap is almost the same.

I read that you can double or triple soap recipes, but you should never attempt to make half or a quarter of a recipe. Why is this?

It sounds like absolute nonsense to me. With the recipes in this book, you can half them, double them, triple them, whatever you like. Weigh the ingredients accurately and you will make good soap. The only difference is that the tracing time may change. (For more information, see page 32.)

Would the soap get ready sooner if I cover it while it is in the molds?

The only advantage I know of covering soap is that it prevents lye from reacting with the air to form a white, powdery layer. (See page 39.)

A friend told me that if I wanted soap to harden more quickly, I could bake it in an oven. What do you think?

I think there's no substitute for time,
to make good soap and fine wine.

All kidding (and bad poetry) aside, even at the lowest oven temperatures (150 to 200 degrees F), soap is likely to crack. If you bake freshly made soap that is still soft, it will *melt!* I suggest that once you take soap from the mold, you allow it to age naturally (at room temperature for the time specified in the recipe). I've found no shortcut.

I've read a lot about soapmaking. One soapmaking book says, "While stirring soap, don't scrape the sides of the container." I've also read that soap might not turn out right if I stir it too quickly or too slowly. What do you say?

I say the soapmakers you read about must have been holding their breath, hoping the soap turned out right! Soap recipes are calculated carefully. Everything that goes in the mixing bowl should come out of the mixing bowl. Scraping the sides of the container is necessary for an even mixture. In fact, I like to stir soap with a rubber spatula just for the reason that it is easy to scrape the sides of the container. As far as stirring soap too quickly or too slowly goes, it doesn't matter. Just relax and follow the recipe.

To add color and fragrance to soap, can I dissolve the lye in rose water or herbal tea instead of plain water?

The concept is good, but the execution is a problem. Anything added to lye must fight for its life. Herbal tea and rose water are too weak to make any noticeable difference in soap.

I use unscented soap because I really can't tolerate fragrance. Can I omit the fragrant oil from your recipes?

You can omit fragrant oil from every recipe, but I can't guarantee the soap will be scent-free. Some fats lend odors to soap. Since you're concerned with fragrances, maybe you're interested in this: I recently read the label of a nationally advertised commercial soap, boldly labeled "unscented." In small print, the list of ingredients included "fragrance."

Can I add color, and maybe fragrance, to soap by adding things from my kitchen like cocoa, turmeric or cinnamon?

Ground spices such as paprika, turmeric and cinnamon can add color to soap, but they are abrasive. Before you add any powder to soap, test it by rubbing it between your fingers. If the powder feels sharp and gritty, then it will feel sharp and gritty in the finished soap. I don't add cocoa or turmeric to soap because of the strong scent they cause.

Do you have a good recipe for saddle soap?

Not in this book. Leather soap and saddle soap aren't really soap at all. They are stiff creams, usually containing beeswax, that are briskly rubbed onto leather to clean and treat it. They are not designed to lather.

If I use something from my kitchen to make soap, can I use it again for cooking?

Lye doesn't affect stainless steel. Lye slightly affects wood and glass. Over time, this can cause permanent etching (frosting) of glass and the gradual wearing away of wood. If you use a container once or twice to make soap, you probably won't notice any damage. If you make multiple batches of soap (which I bet that you will), use the same containers each time and devote them solely to soapmaking.

(From a soapmaking book) The browned pieces of fat that remain after rendering fat are called "cracklings."

Sorry, but cracklings are *not browned pieces of fat*. Cracklings are fried pork rind (skin). To make cracklings, cook pork rind until it is almost wholly rendered of its fat. When the rind becomes crisp and brittle, it crackles when bitten into. Crackling cornbread anyone?

When you put soap in a freezer, aren't you concerned that foods will absorb the soap fragrances?

I haven't noticed a problem. If you worry about it, slip the soap into a plastic bag; secure the bag and then put the soap in the freezer.

I'm an avid gardener and I would like to include fresh herbs and vegetables in soap. Do you have a good recipe?

Fresh plant matter such as herbs and vegetables rot, even when encased in soap. Colors usually fade and so does the fragrance. If you want to add herbs and vegetables to soap, I suggest you dry them first and then grind them to a fine powder.

Can I combine two or three recipes to develop different kinds of soap?

That's an excellent idea! You deserve five stars for fearless creativity! Combine any recipes you desire. Determine the tracing time and the aging time by your soapmaking experiences, rather than by the times stated in the recipes. The possibilities are endless!

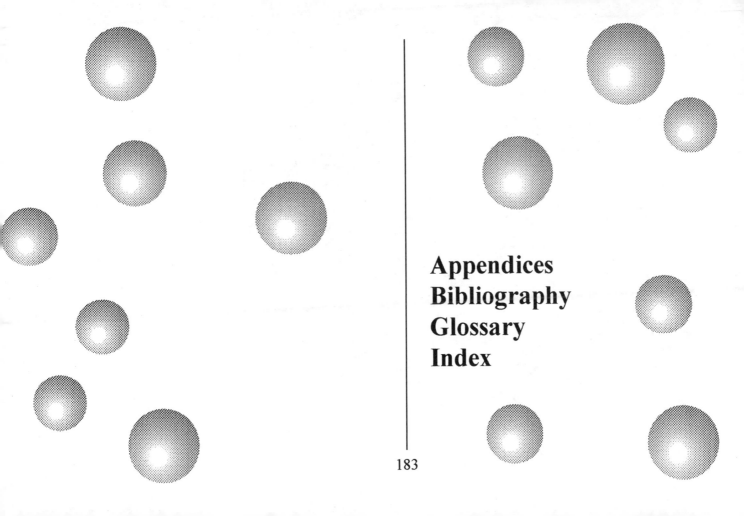

Appendices
Bibliography
Glossary
Index

Appendix A
What is pH?

Technically, pH stands for potential of hydrogen. The scale of pH values goes from 0 to 14. Very strong acids have a very low pH, while very strong alkalis have a very high pH. Pure water is neutral with a pH of 7.

The pH of toilet soap should test between 8 and 10. Soap with a pH of 10 is more harsh to skin than soap with a pH of 8. Do not use soap with a pH higher than 10 for bathing.

pH values of common substances	
muriatic acid	0.0 - 1.0
soft drinks	2.0 - 4.0
lemon juice	2.2 - 2.5
vinegar	2.4 - 3.5
tomato juice	4.0 - 4.5
beer	4.0 - 5.0
chlorine laundry bleach	6.0
milk	6.3 - 6.6
egg white	7.5 - 8.0
soap	8.0 - 10.0
milk of magnesia	10.5
household ammonia	11.0 - 12.0
lye (sodium hydroxide)	13.0 - 14.0

Appendix B
How to determine soap pH

Taste it. Yes, taste it. In the late 1800s, chemists told consumers to test soap with this simple method. Hold the soap to your tongue for a few seconds. If you experience a tingling or burning sensation, the soap is too harsh. Do not use it. You don't like that test? It's simple enough. Well, perhaps a more reliable method is a pH test.

A pH test kit contains strips of chemically treated papers and a color chart. When immersed in a dilute soap solution, the papers react with alkali and change colors. Compare the colors of the strips to the color chart to determine the pH of soap.

(pH test continued)

Step-by-step directions to determine the pH of soap

Step 1: Choose a small glass dish and set it in a sink.

Step 2: Pour distilled water over a bar of soap. Rub the soap as if you were washing your hands.

Step 3: Drip soapy water from your hands and the soap into the dish.

Step 4: Take a pH strip from the kit and wet it with the soapy water in the dish.

Step 5: Match the colors on the strip with the color chart to determine the pH.

Appendix C
Stable scents for soap

bergamot
boise de rose (rosewood)
caraway
cedar wood oil
cinnamon
citronella
clove oil (leaf)
lemon grass oil
neroli (orange flower)
patchouli
peppermint
pimento (allspice)
rosemary
sandalwood
sassafras
spearmint
thyme

Appendix D
How to mix aniline dye to create new colors

Measure the colors and put them into a tiny container; mix well
and use 1/8 to 1/4 teaspoon to color one batch of soap.

New color	Number of 1/8 teaspoons required of these colors			
	Red	Yellow	Blue	Green
turquoise			4	2
brown	7	4		2
grape	5		2	
rose pink	5		1	
lime green		3		1
pistachio green		1		4
orange	2	3		
peach	1	2		
salmon	3	2		
black	4	2	7	

Appendix E
How to render animal fat

Cut the fat into small pieces and put it in a large pot with about two cups water. Do not cover the pot. Cook the fat over medium heat until the water evaporates, the fat pieces turn brown and the liquid fat turns clear. This can take as long as four hours, depending on the amount of fat.

Carefully strain the hot fat and place it in a refrigerator or freezer to harden. (Birds love the solid pieces that remain after you strain the fat.) Lift the hardened fat from the water. Scrape any impurities from the top and bottom of the fat.

Rendered animal fat is called "tallow." It will keep for months in the refrigerator and for years in the freezer. I store tallow, unwrapped in a frost-free freezer. With time, the drying action of the freezer removes water that might remain in the tallow It's impossible to accurately weigh tallow that contains water.

Note: *Do not* add salt, alum, vinegar or lemon juice to tallow in an attempt to improve it. These additives can change the pH of tallow and upset the lye-fat ratio of the soap recipe.

Appendix F
Lake color test results
(See page 48 to read about lake colors.)

Color tested	Color in soap	Stable	Color-fast
yellow	yellow	yes	no
blue	violet to purple	no	no
black	muddy red	no	no
red	muddy red	almost	no
violet	muddy red	no	no
green	brown	no	no
orange	muddy orange	almost	no

Appendix G

How colors react when marbled

See Marbled Soap, page 160.

Soap colors mixed	Effect
yellow and blue	yellow, blue and green
red and blue	red, blue and purple
red and green	red, green, brown and black
blue and orange	blue, orange and gray
yellow and green	yellow, green and light green
yellow and purple	yellow, purple and brown
brown and blue	brown, blue and black
orange and red	orange, red and light red
orange and yellow	orange, yellow and light orange
orange and green	orange, green and yellow-green
orange and purple	orange, purple and reddish brown

Appendix H
Temperature conversion table
(from Fahrenheit to Centigrade)

F	C	F	C	F	C	F	C	F	C	F	C	F	C	F	C
32	0	62	17	92	33	122	50	152	67	182	83	212	100	242	117
34	1	64	18	94	34	124	51	154	68	184	84	214	101	244	118
36	2	66	19	96	36	126	52	156	69	186	86	216	102	246	119
38	3	68	20	98	37	128	53	158	70	188	87	218	103	248	120
40	4	70	21	100	38	130	54	160	71	190	88	220	104	250	121
42	6	72	22	102	39	132	56	162	72	192	89	222	106	252	122
44	7	74	23	104	40	134	57	164	73	194	90	224	107	254	123
46	8	76	24	106	41	136	58	166	74	196	91	226	108	256	124
48	9	78	26	108	42	138	59	168	76	198	92	228	109	258	126
50	10	80	27	110	43	140	60	170	77	200	93	230	110	260	127
52	11	82	28	112	44	142	61	172	78	202	94	232	111	262	128
54	12	84	29	114	46	144	62	174	79	204	96	234	112	264	129
56	13	86	30	116	47	146	63	176	80	206	97	236	113	266	130
58	14	88	31	118	48	148	64	178	81	208	98	238	114	268	131
60	16	90	32	120	49	150	66	180	82	210	99	240	116	270	132

Appendix I
Conversion of US fluid measure to metric

	Fluid Drams	Tea-spoons	Table-spoons	1/4 Cups	Gills 1/2 Cups	Cups	Gallons	Milli-liters	Liters
1 Fluid Dram	1	3/4	1/4	1/16 .0625	.03125	.0156	1/1024	3.7	.0037
1 Tea-spoon	1 1/3	1	1/3	1/12	1/24	1/48	1/768	5	.005
1 Table-spoon	4	3	1	1/4	1/8	1/16	1/256	15	.015
1/4 Cup	16	12	4	1	1/2	1/4	1/64	59.125	.059
1 Gill 1/2 Cup	32	24	8	2	1	1/2	1/32	118.25	.118
1 Cup	64	48	16	4	2	1	1/16	236	.236
1 Gallon	1024	768	256	64	32	16	1	3785.4	3.785
1 Milli-liter	.270	.203 OR 1/5	.068	.017	.008	.004	.0003	1	.001 1/1000
1 Liter	270.5	203.04	67.68	16.906	8.453	4.227	.264	1000	1

Appendix J
Conversion of US weight to metric
For the recipes in this book, determine "ounces" by weight.

	Grains	Drams	Ounces	Pounds	Milli-grams	Grams	Kilo-grams
1 Grain	1	.004	.002	1/7,000	64.7	.064	.0006
1 Dram	27.34	1	1/16	1/256	1,770	1.77	.002
1 Ounce	437.5	16	1	1/16	28835	28.35	.028
1 Pound	7,000	256	16	1	"lots"	454	.454
1 Milli-gram	.015	.0006	1/29,000	1/"lots"	.1	.001	.000001
1 Gram	15.43	.565	.032	.002	1,000	1	.001
1 Kilo-gram	15,430	564.97	.000032	2.2	1,000,000	1,000	1

Appendix K
Suppliers

Alternative Beverage
1400-O Freeland Lane
Charlotte, NC 28217
Telephone: (704) 527-2337
Fax: (704) 527-9643
*thermometers, pH test meter, hops
and bentonite*

Aura Cacia
Post Office Box 399
Weaverville, CA 96093
Telephone: (916) 623-3301
Order line: 1-800-437-3301
Fax: (916) 623-2626
fixed oils and essential oils

Barker Enterprises, Inc.
15106 10th Avenue SW
Seattle, WA 98166
Telephone: (206) 244-1870
Fax: (206) 244-7334
waxes, molds and candle dyes

Betterbee Beekeeping and
Candlemaking Supplies
Route 4, Box 4070
Greenwich, NY 12834
Telephone: (518) 692-9669
pollen, wax and molds

Binder Industries/Candlewic
35 Beulah Road
New Britain, PA 18901
Telephone: (215) 348-1544
Fax: (215) 348-0419
*molds, waxes, candle dyes
and thermometers*

Brushy Mountain Bee Farm
Route 1, Box 135
Moravian Falls, NC 28654
Telephone: 1-800-BEESWAX
waxes and molds

233 46876
7929

Chem Lab Supplies
1060 Ortega Way, Unit C
Placentia, CA 92670
Telephone: (714) 630-7902
Fax: (714) 630-3553
pH kits, pH meters, electronic scales, water test kits, lye, rosin and oils

Dabney Herbs
Post Office Box 22061
Louisville, KY 40252
Telephone: (502) 893-5198
herbs, fixed oils, essential oils, waxes and rosin

Deep Flex Plastic Molds, Inc.
1200 Park Avenue
Post Office Box 1257

$ 5

Murfreesboro, TN 37133-1257
Telephone: (615) 896-1111
Fax: (615) 898-1313

Devonshire Apothecary
Post Office Box 160215
Austin, TX 78716-0215
Telephone: (512) 477-8270
herbs and essential oils

Earth Guild
33 Haywood Street
Asheville, NC 28801
Telephone: 1-800-327-8448
waxes, pH test kits, water test kits, thermometers and clay

$3ᵒᵒ *15ᵇᵗ*
5

Embossing Arts Company
1200 Long Street
Post Office Box 626
Sweet Home, OR 97386
Telephone: (503) 367-3279
Fax: (503) 367-3259
rubber stamps and embossing supplies to decorate soap labels

95411 528-9898
541-529-9917

The Essential Oil Company
Post Office Box 206
Lake Oswego, OR 97034
Telephone: (503) 697-5992
Fax: (503) 697-0615
fixed oils, essential oils and molds

Five Star Stamps
Post Office Box 2121
Southern Pines, NC 28388
Telephone: (910) 692-0950
Fax: (910) 692-0629
*rubber stamps and embossing supplies
to decorate soap labels*

Gold Medal Products Company
2001 Dalton Avenue
Cincinnati, OH 45214-2089
Telephone: (513) 381-1313
Toll-free: 1-800-543-0862
Fax: (513) 381-1570
vegetable oils and coconut oil

Grandma's Spice Shop
Post Office Box 472
Odenton, MD 21113
Telephone: (410) 672-0933
herbs, oils and clay

Hagenow Laboratories, Inc.
1302 Washington Street
Manitowoc, WI 54220
Telephone: (not advertised, please correspond
             by mail)
*rosin, waxes, lye, kaolin, essential oils, pH kits
and thermometers*

Haussmann's Herb and Import Store
534-536 West Girard Avenue
Philadelphia, PA 19123
Telephone: (215) 627-2143
Fax: (215) 627-8943
*herbs, fixed oils, essential oils, waxes
and resins*

Indiana Botanic Gardens
Post Office Box 5
Hammond, IN 46325
Telephone: (219) 947-4040
herbs, fixed oils and essential oils

K & W Popcorn, Inc.
710 East 24th Street
Post Office Box 275
Trenton, MO 64683-0275
Telephone: (816) 359-2030
Fax: (816) 359-3026
*white coconut oil: 1-gallon and
50-pound containers (will ship)*

Lapp's Bee Supply Center
500 South Main Street
Post Office Box 460
Reeseville, WI 53579
Telephone: (414) 927-3848
wax, thermometers and molds

E. C. Kraus
9001 East 24 Highway
Post Office Box 7850
Independence, MO 64054
Telephone: (816) 254-7448
*hops, pH papers, thermometers,
bentonite and sealing wax*

The Lebermuth Company, Inc.
Post Office Box 4103
South Bend, IN 46624
Telephone: (219) 259-7000
Fax: (219) 258-7450
wholesale herbs and essential oils

Lorann Oils
4518 Aurelius Road
Post Office Box 22009
Lansing, MI 48909-2009
Telephone: 1-800-248-1302
Fax: (517) 882-0507
*fixed oils, essential oils, waxes and
candy molds*

Nature's Herb Company
Post Office Box 40604
San Francisco, CA 94140
Telephone: (415) 601-0700 *cell phone?*
herbs, fixed oils and essential oils

Penn Herb Company, Ltd.
603 North Second Street
Philadelphia, PA 19123-3098
Telephone: (215) 925-3336
Fax: (215) 925-7946
herbs, fixed oils, essential oils,
waxes and rosin

Pourette Soapmaking Supplies
6910 Roosevelt Way NE
Post Office Box 15220
Seattle, WA 98115
Telephone: (206) 525-4488
Fax: (206) 525-2795
waxes, molds and candle dyes

Presque Isle Wine Cellars
9440 Buffalo Road
North East, PA 16428
Telephone: (814) 725-1314
Fax: (814) 725-2092
pH test kits, pH meters, bentonite
and scales

Quill Corporation
Post Office Box 94080
Palatine, IL 60094-4080
Telephone: (708) 634-4800
Fax: (708) 634-5708
boxes, electronic scales, plastic bags and a
complete line of office supplies

Robbins Container Corporation
222 Conover Street
Brooklyn, NY 11231
Telephone: (718) 875-3204
boxes, printed packing tissue, tape,
bags and bins

The Rosemary House, Inc.
120 South Market Street
Mechanicsburg, PA 17055
Telephone: (717) 697-5111
herbs, fixed oils, essential oils and henna

Sax Arts and Crafts
2405 South Calhoun Road
Post Office Box 51710
New Berlin, WI 53151-0710
Telephone: 1-800-323-0388
Fax: (414) 784-1176
"Everything your art desires"

Sugar Plum Sundries
5152 Fair Forest Drive
Stone Mountain, GA 30088
Telephone: (404) 297-0158
complete line of soapmaking supplies

Sunfeather Herbal Soap Company
HCR 84 Box 60-A
Potsdam, NY 13676
Telephone: (315) 265-3648

Fax: (315) 265-2902
complete line of soapmaking supplies

Tri-state Theater Supply Company
151 Vance Avenue
Memphis, TN 38103
Telephone: (901) 525-8249
Fax: (901) 733-8249
*white coconut oil: 1-gallon and
50-pound containers (will ship)*

Walnut Acres Organic Farms
Penns Creek, PA 17862
Telephone: 1-800-433-3998
Fax: (717) 837-1146
fixed oils, goat milk and soybean milk

Woodworker's Supply
1108 North Glenn Road
Casper, WY 82601
Telephone: 1-800-645-9292
Fax: (307) 577-5272
pumice, aniline dye, wax and rosin

Bibliography

Bramson, Ann, *Soap: Making it, Enjoying it*. New York: Workman Publishing Company, 1972.

Brannt, W.T., *Manufacture of Soaps and Candles*. Philadelphia, 1888.

Carmichael, John, *A Treatise on Soapmaking*. New York: Collins and Perkins, 1810.

Cristiani, R.S., *A Technical Treatise on Soap and Candles*. Philadelphia: Henry Carey Baird and Company, 1881.

Deite, Carl, *Manual of Toilet Soapmaking*. New York: D. Van Nostrand Company, (no date).

Henley's Formulas for Home and Workshop, Edited by Gardner D. Hiscox. New York: Avenel Books, Revised Edition, 1927.

Hobson, Phyllis, *Making Homemade Soaps and Candles*. Vermont: Garden Way Publishing, 1975.

Hurst, George H., *Soaps: A Practical Manual of the Manufacture of Domestic, Toilet and other Soaps*. London: Scott, Greenwood and Company, 1898.

Maine, Sandy, *Soapmaking and the Creative Art of Business*. Potsdam, New York: Sunfeather, 1995.

Mohr, Merilyn, *The Art of Soapmaking*. Ontario, Canada: Camden House Publishing, 1979.

Bibliography continued

Morfit, Campbell, *A Practical Treatise on the Manufacture of Soaps.*
New York: John Wiley and Son, 1871.

Plummer, Beverley, *Fragrance: How to Make Natural Soaps, Scents and Sundries.* New York: Atheneum, 1975.

Poucher, W.A., *Perfumes, Cosmetics and Soaps.* London: Chapman and Hall, 1974.

Richter, Dorothy, *Make Your Own Soaps, Plain and Fancy.* New York: Doubleday and Company, Inc., 1974.

Rodale's Book of Practical Formulas: Easy-to-Make, Easy-to-Use Recipes for Hundreds of Everyday Activities and Tasks, Edited by Paula Dreifus Bakule. Emmanus, PA: Rodale Press, 1991.

Webb, David A., *Making Potpourri, Colognes and Soaps.* Blue Ridge Summit, PA: Tab Books, 1988.

Wigner, J.H., *Soap Manufacture.* New York: Chemical Publishing Company, Inc., 1940.

Glossary

abrasive, abrasives - Gritty powders in soap to help rub off dirt and dead skin cells.

absolute oil - Highly concentrated perfume which may be liquid, solid or semi-solid; soluble in alcohol; see essential oil.

acid, acidity - A chemical compound containing hydrogen as an essential constituent and which possesses a sour taste; neutralizes alkalis, and combines with bases to form salts.

additive - A soap ingredient not required for saponification; see filler.

age, aging - The time between pouring soap into molds and the time it is ready for use. During this time lye continues to react with the fats; the soap hardens and becomes milder.

alchemy - One of the earliest forms of chemistry. The ancient practice combined science, religion, philosophy and magic.

alcohol - A colorless, inflammable volatile liquid; chemically, any of a class of chemical compounds derived from hydrocarbons.

alkali - Originally the soda derived from the ashes of plants; now, any of various compounds such as sodium hydroxide (lye) which neutralize acids to form salts and turn red litmus paper blue.

alkaline - Having the properties of an alkali.

almond meal - The nutlike kernel of the fruit of the almond tree, *Prunus amygdalus*, coarsely ground as corn is ground to corn meal.

almond paste - The nutlike kernel of the fruit of the almond tree, *Prunus amygdalus*, finely ground to form a paste, as peanuts are ground to form peanut paste, or peanut butter.

aluminum - Chemically an oxidation-resistant white metal with a bluish tinge, and a luster somewhat resembling, but far inferior to that of silver. Reacts with sodium hydroxide (lye).

ammonia - A volatile alkali, a colorless, pungent, suffocating gas; very soluble in water.

aniline - A substance available from indigo and other organic substances, synthetically obtained from nitrobenzene used in dyes, varnish, drugs and resins.

aniline dye - Chemically any of the synthetic dyes obtained from aniline, usually from coal tar.

anise - See licorice.

aphrodisiac - Food or a medicine exciting sexual desire.

aroma - An agreeable odor; fragrance; perfume; bouquet.

aromatherapy - Treatment based on the fact that, when inhaled, certain fragrances can affect the mind and body; practiced since ancient times.

arrow root powder -A tropical American plant, *Maranta arundinacea*, or some other species, whose roots are ground to powder to yield a nutritious starch much used in food preparations.

avocado oil - A fixed, greenish oil from the fruit of a small tree of the laurel family, common in tropical America and the West Indies.

baby oatmeal - A specially-prepared cereal made of precooked oatmeal; sold in powdered form.

baby oil - Mineral oil with the addition of fragrance.

baking soda - Sodium bicarbonate.

barley - The grain or seed of a widely distributed cereal plant of the genus *Hordeum*.

base ingredient - Chemically, a compound which reacts with an acid to form a salt. Lye is a strong base.

batch - Any quantity of a thing made at one time.

bayberry wax - See myrtle wax.

bee pollen - The male element in flowering plants made up of masses of fine, powdery grains or microspores collected by honey bees as a protein food source.

beeswax - The wax secreted by honey bees, of which they construct their honeycomb.

bentonite - Named from Fort Benton, Montana; a rock consisting mainly of clay minerals formed from the decomposition of volcanic ash, capable of absorbing large quantities of water, and capable of being activated by acid: used as an emulsifier in drugs and as a carrier for chemicals.

borax - A white crystalline salt, sodium tetraborate, occurring in nature or prepared artificially: used as an antiseptic, cleansing agent, water softener and as a preservative.

bovine - Oxlike; a bovine animal. A cow is a female bovine animal.

calamus root - The aromatic root of the sweet flag, *Acorus calamus.*

calcium carbonate - Chemically, a colorless crystal or gray powder occurring naturally in calcite, chalk, limestone and marble; used as an antacid and as baking powder. calendula petals - The petals of any plant of the genus *Calendula*, especially *Calendula officinalis*, a common marigold.

callus, calluses - A hardened or thickened portion of skin.

camphor, camphorated - A whitish, translucent, volatile and aromatic crystalline substance, obtained chiefly from the tree *Cinnamomum camphora.*

caprine - Meaning goatlike.

cardamom - The aromatic capsule of various plants of the ginger family, employed in medicine as well as an ingredient in sauces and curries.

carnauba wax (Brazil wax) - Greenish-yellow wax obtained from the Brazilian wax palm.

carrageen - See Irish moss.

casein - A white amorphous phosphoprotein in milk coagulated by acids and lye (sodium hydroxide).

castile soap - Soap made from olive oil which originated in the Castila region of Spain.

castor oil (ricinus oil) - The castor oil plant belongs to the spurge family and fixed oil is obtained from its seeds.

caustic - A caustic substance; as sodium hydroxide capable of burning or destroying animal tissue: sodium hydroxide, caustic potash, potassium hydroxide.

caustic soda - Sodium hydroxide or lye.

chamomile, camomile - Any plant of the genus *Anthemis*, especially *Anthemis nobilis*, an herb with strongly scented foliage and flowers that are used medicinally; any of various allied plants such as *Matricaria chamomilla*, German chamomile.

chlorine laundry bleach - A sodium hypochlorite solution used to whiten laundry and to sanitize floors, walls and other surfaces.

cinnamon - Inner bark of a tree of the laurel family, genus *Cinnamomum*, native to tropical Asia, used as a spice or in medicine as a cordial or carminative; a reddish brown.

cocoa (cacao) butter - The *Theobroma cacao* is a small, evergreen tree cultivated for its seeds, which are used in making cocoa and chocolate. Cocoa butter is a fatty substance pressed from the seeds; solid at room temperature; a good addition to liquid vegetable oils to make a harder soap with better lathering properties.

cocoa powder - Powder prepared from cured, roasted cocoa beans.

coconut oil - The coconut is the fruit of the coconut palm. The coconut seed, one of the largest of all seeds, lies inside the shell, from which a fixed oil is obtained.

color-fast - Keeping its original shade of color without fading in the sunlight or the color running onto other surfaces.

confetti - Narrow streamers or bits of colored paper thrown at weddings, parties and carnivals.

corn meal - Coarsely ground dried corn.

corn oil - A fixed, liquid vegetable oil expressed from corn.

coriander - An annual plant of the carrot family, the seeds of which are aromatic and flavorful and are used in certain liqueurs and in cookery.

créme de la créme - The best of its kind.

curdle - To coagulate; to change into curd.

cure (curing) - The time between pouring soap into molds and the time it is ready for use; also known as aging or texturing-out.

dandelion - A common composite plant, *Taraxacum officinale*, abundant as a weed, characterized by deeply toothed leaves and golden-yellow flowers; any other plant of the genus *Taraxacum*.

decongestant - To relieve an unnatural accumulation of excess fluid in an organ or part; particularly sinus congestion.

detergent - Anything that has a strong cleansing power; a chemical substance or a synthetic preparation having cleansing properties; an oil-soluble substance used in lubricating oil.

distilled water - The volatilization of water by heating in a retort or still and condensing the resultant vapor by cooling; the purification or refinement of a water.

earthnut - See peanut oil.

eclectic - Choosing what seems best; composed of such selections.

elderflowers - Any tree or shrub of the honeysuckle family, genus *Sambucus*, with white flowers and purple berrylike drupes.

emollient - Oils and waxes that soften and soothe skin.

enamel - essential oil (peppermint)

enamel - A substance resembling glass, but differing from it by a greater degree of fusibility or opacity, used as a protective coating for metal; a smooth, glossy surface.

epicurean - Luxurious; given or pertaining to sensual pleasures or luxury.

essential oil - Volatile product from odorous plant material of a single form and species with which it agrees in name and odor. Extracted through water distillation, steam distillation, water and steam distillation or dry distillation:

    Anise - *Pimpinella anisum*
    Bergamot - *Citrus bergamia*
    Bois de rose - The oil of rosewood, *Aniba rosaedora.*
    Camphor (white) - *Cinnamomum camphora*
    Caraway - *Carum carvi*
    Cedar wood - *Juniperus virginiana* or *Juniperus Mexicana*
    Cinnamon - Oil from the bark of *Cinnamomum zeylanicum*
    Citronella - *Cymbopogon nardus*
    Clove (leaf) - *Eugenia caryophylatta*
    Eucalyptus - *Eucalyptus globulus*
    Fir needle oil - *Abies siberiensis*
    Lavender - *Lavandula officinalis, Lavendula vera or Lavendula latifolia*
    Lemon grass - *Cymbopogon citratus*
    Lemon - *Citrus limonum*
    Neroli - *Citrus bigaradia or Citrus arantium.*
    Patchouli - *Pogostemon patchouli or cablin*
    Peppermint - *Mentha piperita*

Pine - *Pinus strobus*
Rosemary - *Rosmarinus officinalis*
Sandalwood - *Santalum album*
Sassafras - *Ocotea cymbarum, Ocotea pretiosa*
Spearmint - *Mentha viridis, Mentha spicata*
Spike (lavender) - *Lavandula latifolia*
Thyme - *Thymus vulgaris or Thymus zygis*
Wintergreen - *Gaultheria procumbens*
Ylang-ylang - *Cananga odorata*

etceteras - A number of other things unspecified; extras or additional items; the rest; and so forth.

extract - Something extracted; a concentrated preparation of a substance that usually contains alcohol.

fat - A soft solid organic compound composed of carbon, hydrogen and oxygen; the tissues of animals and sometimes plants, that contain principally an oily or greasy substance. See fixed oil.

FD & C - An abbreviation for: food, drugs and cosmetics.

filler - A powdered ingredient added to soap to enhance it or to add bulk; not necessary for saponification such as powdered herbs, clay, starches, talc and bark.

fir needle oil - Provides a traditional pine fragrance to soap, air freshener and cleaning products. See essential oil.

fixed oil - Non-volatile fats derived from plant materials. Commonly referred to as vegetable oils. Most commercial vegetable oils are expeller pressed and the remaining material is put through a solvent extraction process and added back to the oil yielded from the pressing.

folk lore - The traditional beliefs, customs, legends and songs of a people that are handed down orally from generation to generation; the study of these traditions.

fragrance, fragrant - The quality of being fragrant; sweetness of smell; pleasing scent; perfume. See essential oil.

fuller's earth - A variety of clay and fine siliceous material, used in absorbing grease from fabric, in fulling and cleansing cloth, and as a dusting powder.

glycerin, glycerine - Chemically, glycerol, an odorless, colorless, syrupy, sweet-tasting liquid compound of the alcohol class obtained by saponification of fats; soluble in alcohol and water.

henna - A tropical plant, *Lawsonia inermis*; a dye made from the leaves of this plant and formerly used to tint hair.

herb - Any plant with a soft or succulent stem which dies to the root every year; any similar plant, especially used in medicines, scents or seasonings.

herbal tea - The dried and prepared leaves and flowers of herbs, from which a beverage is prepared by infusion in hot water; the beverage so prepared.

herbalist - A person who collects plants; a dealer in medicinal plants. A healer who specializes in the curative properties of herbs; also herb doctor.

Hippocrates - A Greek physician born 460 BC.

hydrogenated oil - Chemically to combine, expose to, or treat with hydrogen.

hydrotherapy - Medicinal bathing.

infusion - A liquid extract obtained from a substance by steeping or soaking it in water; any liquid containing organic matter.

Irish moss (carrageen) - A seaweed from the coastal Atlantic, a red algea, *Chondrus crispus*, having cartilaginous tissues from which a carbohydrate emulsifier is obtained and used in foods.

jasmine perfume oil - Synthetic oil with a fragrance similar to jasmine flowers. See essential oil.

lake colors - Liquid, paste and powder used to color foods, drugs and cosmetics.

lanolin, lanoline - An oily or greasy substance obtained from wool, said to be beneficial in skin ointments or lotions.

lard - Lard is rendered pork fat. The small amount of preservatives found in commercial lard doesn't seem to interfere with the soap-making process.

lather, lathering - Foam or suds made from soap agitated with water.

laundry bluing - A blue dye which counteracts yellowness of white fabrics. The color is not stable in soap.

laundry starch - A commercial preparation of plant carbohydrates used to stiffen fabrics in laundering and employed for many industrial purposes.

lecithin - Biochemically, a fatty substance consisting of fatty acids, choline, phosphoric acid and glycerol, found in the cells of plants and animals, and utilized in food, cosmetics and drugs.

lemon balm - A bushy, fragrant perennial mint, *Melissa officinalis*, having lemon-flavored foliage.

lemon grass oil - Provides a traditional lemon fragrance to soap, air freshener and cleaning products. See essential oil.

licorice, liquorice - Sweet-tasting root; extract of *Glycyrrhiza glabra* used in medicine or as a flavoring in confectioneries.

limestone - A rock consisting wholly or chiefly of calcium carbonate, originating principally from the calcareous remains of organisms, and yielding lime when heated.

liquid vegetable oils - Vegetable oils are non-volatile oils pressed from various seeds, fruits and nuts. After being pressed, these oils are refined, bleached and deodorized so thoroughly that the end products are rarely distinguishable from one another by flavor or odor. Oils are 100% fat.

Lorann Oils™ - Trade name of Lorann Oil Company™. The address is on page 198.

lye-water - The amount of lye and water specified in a soap recipe mixed together.

maize - Indian corn; a yellow color similar to the color of ripe corn.

marjoram - Either of two perennial mint plants, *Majorana hortensis*, a sweet and savory herb, or *Origanum vulgare*, pot marjoram, both used for flavor in cooking.

Mentholatum® - Brand name of a chest rub used as a nasal decongestant.

mineral oil (liquid petrolatum) - Any of a class of oils of mineral origin, as petroleum and its derivatives, consisting of mixtures of hydrocarbons, and used as illuminants, fuels, and in certain medicines, as a laxative.

mink oil - Fatty substance obtained from mink fur.

mint - Any plant of the mint family, especially of the genus *Mentha*, comprising aromatic herbs with opposite leaves and small vertically arranged flowers, as the spearmint and peppermint.

monogram - Commonly the initials of a person's name placed on personal items for decoration or identification.

Mother Earth, Mother Nature - Something that gives rise to, or exercises protective care over something else. Exercising control and authority like that of a mother.

mustard powder - Any of several herbaceous plants of the genus *Brassica*, in the mustard family, the seeds yielding the commercial mustard paste or powder; used as a food spice and medicinally for poultices and as a counter-irritant.

myrtle wax - A shrub or tree of the genus *Myrica*, as *Myrica cerifera*, that bears small berries coated with a waxy substance that may be used for making candles; also bayberry, candleberry.

natural-flavor oils - Food-safe, concentrated oils having the aroma and flavor of its name.

oil of bitter almond - Bitter almonds are not edible as they contain poisonous hydrocyanic (prussic) acid. After the acid is removed, the oil is used in flavoring extracts.

olive oil - An oil expressed from the pulp of olives, used with food, in medicine and for soap.

opaque - Not transparent.

optional ingredients - Fillers such as ground herbs and starches added to soap, but not necessary for saponification.

orris root - The rhizome of certain species of *Iris*, as *Iris florentini*, containing an essential oil used as an ingredient in perfumes and medicine, and as a flavoring substance.

palm oil - Palm oil is obtained from the fruit pulp of the oil palm. Palm oil added to vegetable oils makes a harder soap than vegetable oils alone.

peanut oil, earthnut oil - A fixed oil expressed from peanuts.

perfume oil - See essential oil.

Peruvian balsam, Peru balsam, balsam of Peru - Balsam from a leguminous tree of central America used in the manufacture of chocolate, medicine, and perfumes.

petroleum jelly - A thick ointment made of wax and mineral oil.

petroleum products - Products derived from petroleum; mineral oil, baby oil and petroleum jelly.

213

pH - Chemically, the negative of the logarithm of hydrogen ion concentration in aqueous solution: low pH is acid, high pH is alkaline, pH of 7 is neutral.

pH test kit - A kit containing chemically-treated paper and a color chart used to measure the pH of buffered solutions.

pH meter - Electrically operated instrument used to measure hydrogen ion concentration, or pH.

protective film - A thin layer of proteins, oils or waxes that coat the skin and guard against moisture loss.

pumice - A porous, stony substance from volcanoes, lighter than water, used for polishing and smoothing wood, marble, metals and glass.

Pyrex® - Registered trademark of a heat-resistant glass.

Rain Perfume Oil - Soap perfume oil sold by Sunfeather Herbal Soap Company™.

rancid - Having a rank smell or taste; rank or sour-smelling from spoilage, as oils, fats or butter.

ratio - The relation between two similar magnitudes in respect to the number of times the first contains the second, integrally or fractionally. A soap recipe lists the ratio of ingredients.

resin - See rosin (pine).

rev - Colloquialism meaning to increase the speed of; to accelerate.

rice starch - See laundry starch.

rose water - After rose oil is removed from distilled roses, the remaining liquid is called "stronger rose water." An equal volume of distilled water is added to stronger rose water to produce rose water.

rosin - Resin obtained from several varieties of pine trees; used in paint, varnish and soap.

safflower oil - A fixed oil from a thistlelike composite herb, *Carthamus tinctorius*, a native of the Old World, bearing large orange-red flower heads and seeds abundant with oil.

sage - A shrubby methaceous perennial, *Salvia officinalis*, whose grayish-green leaves are used in medicine and for seasoning; also meaning wise; sagacious, judicious and a very wise man.

salt - Chemically, a compound produced by the combination of a base with an acid.

saponify, saponification - The process by which fatty substances, through combination with an alkali, form soap.

scum - The extraneous matter which rises to the surface of liquids in boiling or fermentation; refuse.

sea salt - Salt (sodium chloride) obtained from sea water.

sesame oil - A fixed oil from the seeds of *sesamum indicum*, a tropical, herbaceous plant. For soap, use only the light, colorless sesame oil, not the dark oil made from toasted sesame seeds.

shampoo - To wash, as the hair and scalp, especially with a special solution; to clean with a special substance.

skim milk - Cow's milk with the fat removed.

shortening - Hydrogenated oil is also known as shortening (Crisco® is one brand). Shortenings can contain fat from animals, vegetables or both. Currently, many soapmakers choose to call shortening "vegetable tallow."

soap - A chemical compound of an alkali and fat, soluble in water, and used for cleansing purposes.

sodium bicarbonate - A white crystalline compound used in making baking powder, medical preparations and fire extinguisher liquid. Also baking soda, bicarbonate of soda, saleratus.

sodium hydroxide - A white compound used in manufacturing chemicals, textiles, soap, leather, paper and petroleum products. Also caustic soda, lye, and soda.

soy oil - A fixed, liquid vegetable oil expressed from soybeans, *Glycine max.*

soy milk - Protein-rich liquid expressed from soybeans.

stable (color) - Able to withstand the alkalinity of soap without changing color; resists change and displacement.

stainless steel - An alloy of steel having a small percentage of chromium and other elements which make the steel highly resistant to rust or corrosion.

starch - See laundry starch.

sunflower oil - A fixed, liquid vegetable oil expressed from sunflower seeds.

superfatted - Containing excess fat, oil or emollient.

sweet almond oil - A fixed oil from the edible nuts of the tree, *Prumus amygdalus.*

tallow - The harder and less fusible fat of cattle and sheep, melted and separated from the fibrous or membranous matter for use in candles and soap; a similar fatty substance obtained from plants.

texturing-out - The time between pouring soap into molds and the time it is ready for use; see aging and curing.

thermometer, instant-read - A thermometer that registers the correct temperature within three minutes of inserting it into liquid.

thyme - Any small, aromatic subshrub of the genus *Thymus*, as *Thymus vulgaris* and *Thymus serphyllum*, whose leaves are used as a seasoning in cooking.

tincture - An extract or solution of the active principles of some substance in a solvent, usually alcohol.

trace, tracing, tracing time - A term to describe the consistency (thickness) of soap when it's ready to pour into molds. Tracing time is the length of time soap takes to reach the desired consistency.

turmeric - An East Indian plant of the ginger family, *Curcuma longa*, whose rhizomes are used as a condiment, a yellow dye, and as a chemical test for the presence of alkalis.

USP - United States Pharmacopeia is a book that defines drugs: their properties, the doses safely taken, and standards that determine strength and purity. The US Pharmacopeia is provided by the Food and Drugs Act and is a legal standard. Laws of Congress enforce the requirements of the Pharmacopeia.

valerian- Any of the perennial herbs constituting the genus *Valeriana*, as *Valeriana officinalis*, the garden heliotrope, a plant with white or pink flowers and a root yielding a drug formerly used as a nerve sedative and an agent to check spasms; the drug obtained from the root of *Valeriana officinalis*.

vanillin powder, USP - A white crystalline compound, the active principle of vanilla, extracted from the vanilla bean or prepared artificially from wood pulp.

vegetable oils - See liquid vegetable oils and fixed oils.

vegetable tallow - See shortening.

veggie lover - Colloquialism for a vegetarian or a person who likes to eat vegetables.

Vicks VapoRub® - The registered trademark of a chest rub used as a nasal decongestant.

vinegar - A dilute acetic acid preparation; usually 4 to 8%.

VIP - Abbreviation for: very important person.

vitamin E oil - A vitamin found in wheat germ and other grains; used in treating sterility.

217

volatile oil - Having the quality of passing off quickly by evaporation; able to vaporize freely in the air; apt to change.

walnut oil - A fixed, colorless oil expressed from walnuts; when saponified it causes mottled, brown areas in soap.

wax - A solid, yellowish secretion discharged by bees with which they construct their honeycombs. Any of numerous substances secreted by some plants and animals, as carnauba and spermaceti. Any of various waxlike materials made from hydrocarbon compounds.

wheat germ oil - A fixed oil from the embryo or germ of a grain of wheat; a rich source of vitamin E.

whisk - An stirring implement composed of a bunch of stainless steel loops of wire held together in a handle; used to move with a rapid sweeping stroke.

white coconut oil - See coconut oil.

yellow coconut oil - Coconut oil that contains butter flavor and yellow coloring. See coconut oil.

ylang-ylang (canaga oil) - See essential oil.

zinc - A bluish-white metallic element occurring in combination, used as a protective covering or coating, as a component in alloys, as a reducing agent.

Index